Technocracy in the
European Union

■ POLITICAL DYNAMICS OF THE EU SERIES ■

Series Editors:

**PROFESSOR KENNETH DYSON AND
PROFESSOR KEVIN FEATHERSTONE**

Published Titles:

Legitimacy and the EU

DAVID BEETHAM AND CHRISTOPHER LORD

Forthcoming Titles:

The Common Foreign Security Policy of the EU

DAVID ALLEN

Franco-German Relations

ALISTAIR COLE

A Multi-Speed European Integration Process: Between Hegemony and Dependency?

KEVIN FEATHERSTONE

The Single European Market

ALAN BUTT PHILIP

European Social Policy

MARTIN RHODES

Technocracy in the European Union

CLAUDIO M. RADAELLI

LONGMAN
London and New York

Addison Wesley Longman Limited
Edinburgh Gate
Harlow
Essex CM20 2JE
England
and Associated Companies throughout the world

Published in the United States of America
by Addison Wesley Longman Inc., New York

Visit Addison Wesley Longman on the World Wide Web at:
http://www.awl-he.com

First published 1999

ISBN 0 582 30493 8

British Library Cataloguing-in-Publication Data

A catalogue record for this book is available from the British Library

Library of Congress Cataloging-in-Publication Data

Radaelli, Claudio M. (Claudio Maria), 1960–
Technocracy in the European Union / Claudio M. Radaelli.
    p. cm. — (Political dynamics of the EU series)
Includes bibliographical references and index.
ISBN 0-582-30493-8
1. European Union—Public opinion. 2. Public opinion—European
Union countries. 3. Technocracy. 4. Decision making—European
Union countries. I. Title. II. Series.
HC240.R2 1999
341.242'2—dc21   98-54459
                                                    CIP

Typeset by 35 in 10/12pt Sabon

Printed in Malaysia, LSP

Contents

Series Editors' Preface   vii

Acknowledgements   ix

1   The themes of the book   1

2   From technocratic utopias to the politics of expertise   11

3   Technocracy and European Union public policy making   30

4   The single currency: who won at Maastricht?   53

5   Tax policy in the European Union: technocracy or politicization?   85

6   Media ownership policy: the limits of technocratic regulation   116

7   Conclusions   149

References   157

Index   170

Series Editors' Preface

The decade of the 1990s has been associated with a series of key changes in Europe that have raised major issues for European integration at the start of the new millennium. Some of these changes – the end of the Communist regimes in Eastern Europe, the collapse of the Soviet Union, and German unification – have occurred, of course, outwith the established processes of the European Union. But, in parallel to these changes, the European Union has itself embarked on a major project of both 'widening' and 'deepening', with its agenda dominated by the policies of enlargement and of Economic and Monetary Union. The 'deepening' of the integration process has, in turn, provoked a public backlash in some member states of the EU, as evidenced in the ratification debates on the Maastricht and Amsterdam treaties. In short, the EU faces a period of external challenge, internal reform, and public uncertainty of an unprecedented magnitude.

With this in mind, the emphasis of this new series is very much on the dynamics of the European Union. Together, each of the volumes will analyse and reflect on the implications of such changes for the European integration process in the next decade.

The series also seeks to encourage undergraduate students to reflect theoretically on the implications of these changes. Just how adequate are different analytic frameworks for understanding what is happening in a given area of integration? The series will usefully complement more descriptive and institutionally-based accounts of European integration. At the same time the editors avoid imposing a single theoretical approach on what they recognize to be a wide-range of varying experiences across different areas.

In addition to encouraging theoretical reflection, the series seeks to give a strong empirically-grounded content to each volume in the form of brief case studies, which are designed to illustrate important aspects of the phenomenon under investigation. These case studies focus in particular on the theme of power: of where power lies and of how it is exercised.

Finally, the series encourages authors to reflect on scenarios for development in the policy field or issue area with which they are concerned. In this way, the theoretical and empirical foci of the volumes are brought together.

This second volume in the series is an ideal complement to the first, *Legitimacy in the European Union* by David Beetham and Christopher Lord. The questioning of the legitimacy of the European integration process stems, in large part, from the perception that, for much of its history, the European Union has been designed according to a technocratic ethos. The conception of Jean Monnet emphasised the utility of a technocratic policy leadership, embodied first in the High Authority of the European Coal and Steel Community and then in the Commission. The present volume argues that, in reality, 'technocracy' is counter-balanced by a process of 'politicization' in today's European Union. This increased politicization appears part of the process of system development, as the EU establishes a stronger presence in core areas of political debate. The challenge, however, is to explore new forms of accountability, transparency and regulatory credibility in an environment in which old-style parliamentary politics appear unsuited and unwanted. The intensification of the European integration process, the prospect of the entry of new and poorer members, and the likelihood of a more flexible pattern of participation in EU policies certainly make this challenge topical and acute. This volume offers the reader an invaluable guide to the precise contours of the 'technocracy' problem in the EU. It also illustrates the value of a 'policy analysis' perspective in addressing problems of the EU.

Professor Kenneth Dyson
Professor Kevin Featherstone
University of Bradford

Acknowledgements

This book originated from a proposal of the series editors, Kenneth Dyson and Kevin Featherstone, to contribute to their series with a volume on technocracy. Since then, they assisted me with enthusiasm and perceptive comments throughout the entire book project. I wish to thank them for their effort and their patience. At different stages of the project, Fulvio Attinà', Philipp Genschel, Adrienne Heritier, Phil McGuin and Lucio Pench provided comments and constructive criticisms. Amy Verdun sent me a long e-mail report on Chapter Four. It was of invaluable help in re-drafting this chapter. My dearest Alison was also a great professional partner in this adventure, as shown by her contribution to Chapter Six. Finally, Chris Harrison at Longman gave me unlimited support and professional advice. Criticisms and suggestions saved me from many mistakes, but the final product is entirely my responsibility.

I experimented with the draft manuscript in the 1997–98 academic year. MA students taking my course on Policy Dynamics in the EU Policy Process raised a number of issues concerning policy legitimacy and technocracy. Their feedback was very important as one of the aims in this project is to assist MA seminar groups with conceptual elements and case study material.

Research (especially but not exclusively Chapter Five) was funded by the Economic and Social Research Council (grant R000222059) and, for Chapters Two and Three, the Nuffield Foundation (grant SOC/100/001577 on 'The politics of expertise'). I wish to gratefully acknowledge these two grants.

Much of the final drafting of this book took place at the Robert Schuman Centre of the European University Institute in Fiesole (Italy). I would like to thank the Robert Schuman Centre Director, Yves Mény, for welcoming me as a Jean Monnet Fellow between

January and July 1998. The Robert Schuman Centre provided an extraordinary learning environment, and the hills of Mugello a great place for thinking, hiking, jogging and dining the Italian way.

I wrote the first pages of the book in Milan during the typical hot and humid summer days of late July 1997. I spent those days literally barricaded at my parents' in splendid isolation, with air-conditioning permanently on. The only presence in the day was that of my mother Luisa, who commented on the early conceptual grid of the project when watering the agonized plants she had on the balcony. One day the water spilled over the mind map I had designed as a major reference for the project, but we rescued it. The water stain on the map still reminds me of those intense days in which I appreciated once again my mother's intelligence and spirit. I am privileged to have read the 'book' of her life, and I hope I will read ever more of it. I dedicate this book to her.

Milan, Fiesole and Bradford, September 1998

CHAPTER ONE

The themes of the book

The political system of the European Union (EU), notably the European Commission, is in the firing line. At stake is the allegation of being a political system ruled by technocrats who ignore the basic thrust of democracy. Whilst democracy is based on legitimate consensus, free elections and participation, technocracy recognizes expertise as the sole basis of authority and power.

Complaints about the 'mandarins of Europe' are not new, but in the past Brussels had been able to make public policy in relative isolation from the ordinary citizen. The policy process was managed smoothly, and the citizen did not care much. Europeans differed in the degree of Euro-enthusiasm according to their nationality, but more fundamentally they were not obsessed with what was going on in Brussels and how democratic it was. The salience of 'Europe' was indeed low.

Things changed at the beginning of the 1990s. It all started with the ratification of the Treaty of Maastricht, an impenetrable maze (at least to the layman, but even experts conceded that the quality of the document in terms of standards of good legislation was poor) of technical provisions. But the political message – a single currency for Europe – was clear and citizens had to decide whether they were prepared to swallow it or not. In 1991 the Danes said no, and one year later, in France, the single currency proposal went through the electorate by a narrow margin. The press commented that 'The Danish referendum has exposed the gulf between the Europe planned by the technocrats and heads of states and the Europe of the people – a point Mr Jacques Delors, the European Commission president and arch-federalist, now concedes'.[1] In France, 57 per cent of those who voted 'no' to the Treaty of Maastricht cited 'opposition to technocrats in Brussels'.[2]

Mr David Williamson, the then Secretary General of the Commission, agreed that 'ever since Danish voters rejected the Maastricht Treaty on European political and monetary union last June, it has suited friend and foe alike to single out the Commission as a power-hungry, centralising technocracy'.[3] Governments started to capitalize on these feelings. Jacques Chirac entered his presidential campaign with a political pamphlet, *La France Pour Tous*, wherein he stated flatly that he did not believe in a Europe of technocrats. In his own words: 'Je ne crois pas à une Europe fabriquée à Bruxelles par des technocrates sans légitimité' (Chirac 1994: 105). Quite correctly, the *Financial Times* observed in the wake of presidential elections in France that 'certainly many people, young and old, who voted for Chirac do not intend to replace the demons of socialism with the disadvantages of sinking into an anonymous European Union run by technocrats'.[4]

Even the historical decision to launch the single currency with eleven participants taken at Brussels in May 1998 failed to impress public opinion, presumably puzzled by the row over the presidency of the European Central Bank. Yet the 'lack of a real sense of history in the making' – as the press put it – indicated a deep-rooted apathy which 'should be a cause for concern. For gone are the days when EU politicians could take decisions about the future without involving their citizens in the process'.[5]

In addition, European governments have learnt a very profitable 'blame game' that does not help the cause of EU legitimacy. Although national policy makers are ultimately responsible for adopting EU decisions in the Council of Ministers, they have often blamed the European Commission for domestic decisions difficult to sell to their electorates. It has also been argued that the participation in the EU policy process has altered the balance of forces within domestic political systems between technocrats and politicians.[6] The domestic political impact of the Treaty of Maastricht provides the best illustration of this phenomenon. Countries such as France, Italy, Germany and Spain have been struggling with the convergence criteria established by the Treaty of Maastricht. In these countries, the reform of the welfare state and the tax system has been undertaken with the aim of achieving the objective of monetary convergence. Experts in charge of monetary and macroeconomic policy have gained tremendous power from the EU-driven change of domestic economic policy. In Rome, an elite of technocrats working in the Treasury and the Bank of Italy found in the Treaty of Maastricht sufficient ammunition to tame what was perceived as the most powerful party system of the West (Dyson and Featherstone 1996a). Although Greece was not concerned with reaching the single currency in the first wave, the political activity of 'the pro-European technocrats in charge of economic policy'[7] has been intense. Concluding on this point, the impact of the alleged technocratic system at work in Brussels has been profound in member states too.

Political scientists have detected a dramatic increase in the political power of expertise, well beyond the domain of EU politics and monetary policy. According to Robert Putnam, administrative elites (especially senior civil servants trained in natural sciences and technology) tend to 'agree that "politics" should be replaced by "rationality" . . . although on practical issues they may rarely agree which policy is uniquely "rational"' (Putnam 1977: 409). Andersen and Burns (1996: 244) debunk the 'established political mythology' according to which parliamentary institutions are the core of modern governance. The reality, instead, is one of *post-parliamentary governance*, where experts, large organizations, sectoral networks with the involvement of public and private actors represent the essence of modern governance. A question then arises: is technocracy getting a hold of the policy-making process?

Turning to the EU again, technocracy is not confined to the single currency. It is sufficient to mention the creation of the single market, a plethora of technical measures devised with the aim of assuring the free movement of capital, goods and people. The problem is that trade and capital have been substantially liberalized in the EU, with citizens' freedom of movement as a laggard in this process. Accordingly, citizens do not quite feel the benefits of the single market. The European Commission has (somewhat belatedly) launched the 'Citizens First' programme to make sure that the ordinary citizen appreciates the benefits of the single market, but the truth is that the process is one in which citizens have been least involved. In 1997 the periodical survey *Eurobarometer* suggested that people were not aware of their rights when moving from one member state to another. Many did not know of their right to vote in local elections in the country of residence, and 32 per cent held the false belief that there was an 'EU telephone number' for emergency services.[8] This adds to the perception of a technocratic political system designed with only big capital and trade in mind.

3

European Union decisions have gone further than neutral measures for the smooth functioning of a single market. Currently, Brussels (the European Commission) and Strasbourg (the European Parliament) discuss fundamental ethical issues relating to biological engineering and the future of the human species. The decision-making system of the EU relies on a plethora of working groups, standardization bodies, and committees of experts (Egan 1998; Joerges *et al.* 1997; Pedler and Schaefer 1996; Schmidt and Werle 1998). Thus it is customary to read in the press that, as the *Independent* put it, 'a band of technocrats will assess the "morality" of granting the first European patent on a genetically engineered animal'. The comment went on to suggest that:

> tomorrow, the Book of Genesis will be rewritten. In the unlikely setting of the European Patent Office in Munich, a group of international civil servants will decide whether living animals are part of the natural world or whether they can be artefacts – 'inventions' created by human ingenuity.[9]

Not only citizens, but also companies have occasionally shown hostility towards the EU. A few years ago, Jacques Calvet, chairperson of PSA Peugeot Citroen, in a letter to the *Financial Times* wrote:

> the centralisation of power leads away from democracy. National parliaments are incapable of keeping track of the twists and turns of decisions of a handful of experts. Day in and day out, these technocrats alter economic realities that none of them understands or cares about.[10]

Companies feel that legislation is funnelled through the EU policy process without appropriate consultation and with an underestimation of the impact of European rules on firms, particularly small and medium enterprises.[11] Inside the European Commission the problem is acknowledged as real. A senior British diplomat and head of a Commission cabinet in the 1980s has assessed the period 1985–95 (when the entrepreneurial Jacques Delors was head of the Commission) with the following words:

> There were a lot of bright young things carried on the wave of Delors's power and influence. There were many high-class brains, but there was also culture of arrogance. The Commission believed it represented the pure strain of visionary European thinking. There was a smugness and a disdain for the expression of national concerns.[12]

The recent Treaty of Amsterdam contains an entire title on the quality of EU legislation. Good legislation requires consultation, regulatory impact assessment, and systematic evaluation of the results achieved by European public policies. But it also requires transparency. Mr Jean-Claude Piris, in 1994 head of the European Council's legal service (that is, the EU's senior lawyer in Brussels), stated that 'decision making in the European Union has become so complex that it is impossible for the ordinary citizen to understand'.[13] Paradoxically, the 1996–7 intergovernmental conference in charge of Treaty revision was itself a veritable labyrinth for the European citizen. Two comments from the press give an idea of how the conference proceeded. The first comment refers to the start-up of the conference and is worth quoting at length:

> The Maastricht treaty review conference, which opens today in Turin, is being billed as a chance to shape Europe for the 21st century. Leaders attending the launch ceremony in Lingotto – a Fiat car factory converted into a space-age conference centre – will have a set-piece exchange, lunch, and jet out of town. Then, it's over to the technocrats. For the next few months, almost all the serious preparation of 'Maastricht II' will be in the hands of near-anonymous constitutional experts meeting every week or so in Brussels to discuss possible revisions to the treaty. The process – known as an intergovernmental conference or IGC – involves rolling negotiations between a group of around 20 national representatives with staff support. These one- and half-day sessions are interspersed by meetings of foreign ministers and six-monthly summits between the 15 EU heads of government, where the grand bargains are struck. Maastricht I was widely condemned as an elitist exercise in which politicians and Brussels technocrats delivered a text which was about as dull as a London bus timetable. Yet Maastricht II risks being much the same, for all the promises of greater openness and transparency in the negotiations. Much of it concerns fine-tuning of legal instruments and decision-making.[14]

At the end of the conference, these predictions were confirmed. Even the Italian press, usually enthusiastic about European affairs, provided a rather gloomy assessment of the Amsterdam draft Treaty, arguing that:

> Only the single currency has survived, apparently, in the massacre of ambitions. It was left standing alone with its algid anti-deficit stability pact, without any serious economic counterbalance, without the consensus of the Europe of the people and the unemployed.[15]

In conclusion, there is prima-facie evidence pointing to widespread technocracy in the EU. However, a number of questions must be addressed if the issue of EU technocratic policy making has to be taken seriously. First, what is technocracy and how does it operate? Second, what are the limitations (both from an empirical and a normative point of view) of technocracy? Third, why is it contended that the EU is a technocratic political system? Fourth, does the empirical analysis of EU public policy corroborate or falsify the statement that the EU is a technocracy?

This book tackles these questions step by step. Analysis must proceed beyond anecdotal evidence of the type mentioned above. This requires an examination of the key concept, technocracy. Hence, Chapter Two is dedicated to the fundamental characteristics of technocracy. Different authors have provided alternative (although not incommensurable) definitions of technocracy. Accordingly, Chapter Two will review succinctly the evolution of the concept and highlight the basic elements of technocracy. As technocracy comes, etymologically, from *tekhnē* (art) and *kratos* (power), I will first offer a broad definition of technology based upon the idea of rational methodologies for the organization and control of human activities.[16] If technology is the core element of power, it should not be restricted to machines or to the workplace. Second, I will illustrate the three dimensions of technocracy. Indeed, technocracy is the product of social transformations (the emergence of professionalism, and perhaps of a new 'class' of experts), techno-economic change, and, most crucially, a new form of power. For the purposes of this book, it is the third dimension, that is, the new politics of expertise, which deserves priority. Drawing upon an extensive literature, which goes from Bacon and Saint-Simon to contemporary writers, I will argue that technocratic politics changes the nature of power in that knowledge becomes the terrain of politics (Fischer 1990: 173). Most of the analysis of technocracy has been conducted in a sociological perspective, but for the aim of this book the political implications of the rule of expertise are of paramount importance. In a nutshell, technocratic politics is cemented in the conviction that the chaotic pluralist democracy, where pressure groups, mass movements and self-interested politicians divert the political system from the common good, can be formally respected but must be substantially overtaken by the rules of knowledge and rationality. No technocrat, nowadays, argues that Parliaments should be suppressed or converted in academic senates, but they claim that a vast number of policy areas should be insulated from the 'mess' of democratic policy making.

This claim is fundamentally flawed from a normative point of view. Politics has to do with values, and no algorithm will ever provide an answer to the puzzle of confronting values. In addition, technical rationality is only one type of rationality, and democracy needs normative rationality as well. Not only do technocratic claims present normative drawbacks, they are also empirically weak. The social sciences are still coping with uncertainty over basic mechanisms of political and social life (Lindblom 1990). Even the natural sciences are still in search of answers to the puzzles addressed by public policy. Briefly, the main conclusion in Chapter Two will be that technocracy cannot work. Another conclusion will be that, albeit with exceptions, exaggerations and bias have plagued the literature on technocracy. Typically, writers in this field talk about the technocratic utopia, or, at the opposite, warn of the dangers caused by an all-mighty technocracy. What is lacking is an accurate analysis of public policy making. Unsurprisingly then, writers working on public policy analysis have found more nuanced answers to the questions of the power of technocracy. Accordingly, this body of literature (policy analysis) will be employed at length in the remainder of the book.

Chapter Three will take the analysis of technocracy into a new field, that is, the EU. Although, as we have already seen, allegations of technocratic policy making are rife in the press (and more importantly in public opinion) so far a systematic analysis of the EU in terms of technocracy has not been conducted. There are several reasons for looking at the EU from the angle of technocracy. For one, the institutional structure of the EU presents (a) a bureaucracy (the European Commission) endowed with a pivotal position in policy formation; (b) the lack of a democratically elected government with a legislative programme; (c) a party system still in consolidation, hence comparatively weak; and (d) the proliferation of non-majoritarian institutions (that is, institutions which are not accountable to the political system, for example the European Central Bank). For another, studies of policy making have underlined the relative specialization of the EU in technical policies, especially regulation, and the importance of communities of experts and *copinage technocratique* between the Commission's officials and experts.

One of the main conclusions of Chapter Three will be that technocracy sheds light on important elements of the EU policy process. However, we need to turn to more finely grained concepts – mainly developed by policy analysts: for example, bureaucratic politics, epistemic communities, and advocacy coalitions – for understanding how knowledge plays a role in EU public policy. Not only has the concept of technocracy severe limitations when applied to national political systems, but its explanatory power remains low when applied to the EU. This is due, in essence, to the sweeping generalizations and the inadequately bold arguments sustaining the notion of technocracy.

After having assessed the potential of technocracy for the study of the EU public policy and having discussed other conceptual alternatives (to reiterate, alternatives based on theories of the policy process), the second part of the book will present and discuss three case studies. A sound methodology designed for investigating whether the EU is a technocracy or not – I believe – should include an empirical study of different policy areas. If one of the main problems with technocracy as a concept and tool for analysis is the presence of broad generalizations obfuscating the crucial details of public policy making, an alternative is to generate variability by looking at different policy areas. As averred, the EU has specialized in regulatory policy, whereas distributive policies have been less important. In the case of national political systems the main emphasis of studies on technocracy has been on distributive policy (for example, the function played by the state in sustaining the growth of the military-bureaucratic complex). But technocracy in the EU should be examined within the context of the construction and the regulation of the single market. This is why I have decided to detect the presence of technocracy in EU policy domains different from technology policy (Peterson 1995a). This is also consistent with the broad conceptualizations of technology and technocracy outlined above.

Accordingly, Chapters Four, Five and Six will be dedicated to Economic and Monetary Union, direct tax policy and media ownership regulation. The single currency is the most developed of the three policies, whereas direct tax policy, although the Commission has been active with proposals since the 1960s, has not progressed much. Media ownership regulation, instead, is a new territory for EU institutions, and the policy process here is in its earlier stages. So far the European Commissioner for the single market has presented only a draft for a directive to be discussed by the College of Commissioners. But the ideas of the Commission have already been discussed at length by the other European institutions because of their political potential. The three case studies will offer insights into technocracy at work and Chapter Seven will draw a number of conclusions. My argument will be that there are several technocratic components in the EU policy process, yet the three policies examined in this study deviate from the technocratic pattern in one important respect. In fact, there is evidence of deep politicization in media policy and monetary policy. The relative opacity and insulation of these two areas have been radically challenged by politicians, governments, parliaments and public opinion. The cultural and political challenges to the single currency are indeed the most fundamental ingredient of Europe's road towards a sustainable Euro. In tax policy there is not a similar challenge to technocrats from exogenous actors such as the ordinary citizens or domestic parliaments[17], but in this case the European Commission itself is seeking to promote a more political discourse, following the disappointment of many years of technocratic discourse with poor results.

Politics is then taking precedence over technocracy: the EU has now become less efficient than in the past, but this is the price to pay in a process of polity formation. Indeed, the EU is a maturing political system, and politicization is nothing but the result of political dimensions and conflicts structuring a polity in consolidation. All the same, knowledge and power are deeply intertwined in EU public policy. Although technocracy is not the best characterization of the EU, knowledge remains a crucial terrain of EU public policy. The new challenge for the EU is therefore how to combine an increased politicization with the need for more expertise. Politics and knowledge, which the conventional literature on technocracy sees as polar opposites, are indeed needed at the same time for developing public policy in the EU.

Notes

1 *Financial Times*, 18 September 1992/Enterprise in extremis: The outlook for European union is bleak, whatever the outcome of the French referendum.

2 *Financial Times*, 22 September 1992/Europe's tactical time-out: Resolving the problems which are confronting the EC will take more than a summit meeting.

3   *Financial Times*, 25 September 1992/The ERM and Maastricht: Commission finds itself under siege.

4   *Financial Times*, 16 May 1995/Chirac in the new order.

5   *European Voice*, 30 July–5 August 1998, Editorial comment: Pause for thought.

6   There is a lively debate on this. Among the others, see Dyson and Featherstone (1996a) and Moravcsik (1998).

7   *Financial Times*, 14 November 1994/Survey of Greece.

8   *Eurobarometer*, no. 47, Spring 1997.

9   The *Independent*, 20 November 1995/Is this the work of man or nature?

10 *Financial Times*, 30 April 1992/Personal view: The new utopias that threaten Europe.

11 This has spawned a debate on the quality of EU regulation and regulatory reform at the EU level (Radaelli 1998).

12 The *Independent*, 28 March 1996/The future of Europe: Brussels barons fall on hard times.

13 *Financial Times*, 14 February 1994/Call to open up European maze: Decision-making now too complex for ordinary citizens to understand.

14 *Financial Times*, 29 March 1996/European Law: Talk, lunch – then it's up to the backroom boys.

15 *Il Sole–24Ore*, 19 June 1997, Adriana Cerretelli, Moneta blindata alla tedesca senza riforme e unione politica. (Translation: Armoured currency, the German way. Neither reform nor political union.)

16 A concise overview of different approaches to technology is provided by Schmidt and Werle (1998).

17 See, however, the confrontation between the German and British governments (in Winter 1998) over how far should EU tax policy go. Several British newspapers dedicated the front page to tax coordination, and the issue was debated by parliaments across Europe.

CHAPTER TWO

From technocratic utopias to the politics of expertise

As we muddle through the last quarter of the twentieth century, we find ourselves uneasily, and often hazily, placed between these two extremes: a government of non-experts over experts, or a government planned out by experts without democracy. If democracy is to survive, it will have to steer clear of either extreme.

(Sartori 1987: 431)

Introduction: the key questions

What is technocracy? How does it operate? How can it be assessed? These are topical questions in the analysis of technocracy. Scholars have been engaging with them for more than two centuries. One of the aims of this chapter is to review and assess the basic ingredients of technocratic thought, not for presenting yet another synthesis of the literature (Burris 1993; Fischer 1990; Williams 1971 contain excellent surveys of technocratic ideas), but, rather, for discussing how different authors have shed light on the *political* consequences of the rise of technocrats. This study is concerned primarily with technocracy in public policy. The main emphasis, therefore, is on how expertise and the 'rule by experts' shape the making of public policy. Accordingly, the sociological and organizational characteristics of technocracy are less important here than they would be in a comprehensive review.

To anticipate the answer to the question of 'what is technocracy' in a few, concise words, technocracy is a political regime rooted in the social and economic transformations typical of contemporary societies with a high level of economic development.

11

The economy must have reached a pivotal position in society if the concept of technocracy has to achieve some meaningful connotation. To illustrate: growth must be the most important governmental goal. Although technocratic utopias are as old as capitalism (or even older, if one decides to include Plato's guardianship within the set of technocratic utopias), technocracy manifests itself in societies which have organized their basic institutions (especially the firm, public administration, and the state, but also professions such as teachers and lawyers) around rational methods, efficiency, and 'technically oriented modes of reason and action' (Fischer 1990: 61). Technocracy is all about organization and planning: for Burris, indeed, it is a type of organizational control (Burris 1993). Put differently, technocracy has more to do with organization than with machines, more with systematic approaches to objectives than with specific techniques, and more with efficiency and rational decision making than with technological determinism. Additionally, social transformations include, at least according to certain authors, the emergence of a new class.

However, technology should not be overlooked, particularly if understood in broad terms, as to include organizational technologies (both in the private and the public sector) and technologies of power (Foucault 1980). The essential economic transformation of technocratic societies is indeed technical change: rapid change of technology, technological complexity and organizational interdependence (the literature underlines the idea of the socio-economic *system*) are the fundamental traits of a technocratic economy (Fischer 1990).

At any rate, from the perspective of political science the key question is what are the main *political* consequences of these socio-economic transformations? What is politics in a technocratic society? Does politics turn into government of science or government of scientists? What does the power of technocrats consist of, influence or the power to take decisions? And finally, what is the relationship between experts and politicians? As will be shown below, the literature on technocracy raises more questions than convincing answers to these issues. This literature is flawed because of too many ambiguities. The problem is compounded by a frequent emphasis on prediction (occasionally, the literature is disturbingly fatalistic) and prescription. For this reason, it will be necessary to turn to public policy analysis (a literature partly intertwined with, but independent from, the key arguments of the technocratic literature) for a better understanding of political dilemmas. Political theory will also provide useful insights for assessing normatively the concept of technocracy. It is useful, however, to proceed systematically. The essential themes of technocratic ideas will be illustrated first, and then an assessment will be suggested.

The technocratic project: historical excursus

The technocratic agenda saw the light with the enthusiasms, characteristic of the Enlightenment, for the power of reason, science, and technique (Burris 1993: 21). To be sure, most of contemporary social scientists, including harsh critics of technocracy, believe in rationality and in the contribution of science to contemporary society. Hence what is at stake here is not rationality, but Reason with a capital letter, defined by Sartori as 'the scientistic-physicalist variety of rationalism, its self-assurance, arrogance, and, ultimately, limitless appetite' (Sartori 1987: 437). In any case, much earlier than the eighteenth century, the political philosophy of Plato had already hinted at technocratic ideas. Plato envisaged a political community governed by philosopher-kings, an ideal political system wherein decisions had to be entrusted to the knowledgeable. Dahl, in his study on nuclear weapons and decision making, has dubbed this view guardianship because democracy is put in the hands of 'guardians' who, supposedly, know what is best for us in technical, complex areas of decision making, such as, for example, nuclear weapons (Dahl 1985). The concept of technocracy cannot be stretched to Plato's utopia. For one reason, when Plato was conceiving of his political thought, the economy was not a key element of society. By contrast, a technocratic society revolves around economic imperatives, especially growth and system maintenance. For another, the philosopher of Plato's guardianship was not a master of technique, but a man of ethics and wisdom, capable of infusing direction to society by employing the power of myth and philosophy. The king, according to Plato, had to love *sophia* (knowledge), not science. Sartori adds:

> *Sophia* was, above all, wisdom; whereas we do not ask of a scientist to be wise. Also, philosophy, from the Greeks all the way to the idealists, was the 'knowledge of all things'. The scientist has no knowledge of all things; he is, and must be, a specialist and often a narrow one.   (Sartori 1987: 435)

If a precursor has to be found, this can be Francis Bacon, who in 1627 published his *New Atlantis*, a political utopia where the scientist had replaced Plato's philosopher. With Bacon a technocratic theme appeared, that is the idea of using scientific administration in lieu of politics. In the *New Atlantis* the ruling scientists, called 'fathers' and rigorously male, were to govern for the common good by following science. There is no conceptualization of politics in Bacon: politics is suppressed, not theorized. In addition, there is no economic analysis: as he lived in the eighteenth century, Bacon could not see the industrial organization of society and the rise of technocrats at the top of it. Simply put, there was no such thing as the industrial organization of society in a precapitalist economy. As the economy is a fundamental ingredient of technocratic thought, Bacon can be considered a precursor rather than the father of technocracy.

The founding fathers of technocratic thought are Auguste Comte and Claude-Henry de Saint-Simon.[1] Saint-Simon had a fundamental intuition. Capitalism was still in its infancy, but the French sociologist did not overlook a trend that was to become increasingly important in our century. The key political and economic resource – he noticed – was not the private property of the means of production, but competency. The bourgeoisie and the entrepreneurial heroes of capitalism had been hegemonic in the earlier stage of the modern economy, but – Saint-Simon observed – the future of society was in a general planning capable of delivering the highest utility to the highest number of people. Hence, domination should be distributed according to knowledge and enlightenment, not according to property. France – argued Saint-Simon – would turn into a 'lifeless corpse' if the enlightened elite of society were to disappear, but hardly anybody would notice the loss of the aristocracy.

To illustrate with a few, stark contrasts. Instead of 'animal spirits' (this is the famous definition of capitalist attitudes offered by John M. Keynes) and 'creative destruction' (this is the chaotic process of innovation which, according to Joseph Schumpeter, is generated by entrepreneurial action), the smooth government provided by the plan and rational decision making. Instead of the power of man over man (this being politics), the power of man over nature (this being scientific governance). Instead of self-interested politicians, obedience to the dictates of science. One step forward and – as Sartori observed (1987: 436) – we enter Marxism, with Engels fantasizing about the replacement of the government of men over men by the 'administration of things'. Finally, instead of politicians, *directeurs* (Comte) and *industriels dirigeants*. This is what the founding fathers of technocracy called *dépolitisation*.

Saint-Simon hastened to add that this was the future. The present, by contrast, was a reality wherein the idle still dominated over the most educated and capable individuals. Society was divided into competent professionals and parasites, or, to use the language of classical political economy, productive and unproductive labour. This analysis thus lends itself to class conflict, or at least to a fragmentation of society along class lines. As a consequence, Saint-Simon argued for a radical reorganization of society. With these considerations, a number of extremely important aspects of technocracy had been put in place. To begin with, the argument that competence, rather than property, is the key resource in developed economies. Second, the legitimacy of the rule by experts. Technocrats – the technocratic gospel resonates – should dominate because they are the most capable and most productive members of society. In a single word, meritocracy. The point to stress is that *technocracy is not just organization, it is also ideology and rationalization*. The symbols of competence, expertise and disinterested love of knowledge are powerful rationales within the political agenda of technocracy. Third, the technocratic agenda contains a project of radical change: society and politics must be reorganized, and indeed Saint-Simon is considered a typical utopian socialist. This means that sociological analysis turns into political action, at least in the utopian scenario of Saint-Simon.

But there is another political intuition in Saint-Simon and Comte. In fact, they understood that *dépolitisation* entailed a huge risk, that is the risk of assigning priority to materialistic values. Politics as we know it is not only about power, it is also a conflict of values, beliefs, even ethical choices. As such, it contributes to the moral fabric of society. A purely technocratic society is – to paraphrase Max Weber – an unbearable iron cage. The solution to the dilemma of giving more power to the experts and yet curbing the materialistic trend of technocratic politics was eventually found in the old, medieval distinction between spiritual and temporal power (Burris 1993: 23 and especially Fisichella 1997: 33–5). Managers were to be assigned temporal power, but spiritual power (not command: Comte warned that real theoretical power manifests itself through recommendations and suggestions, never through command) had to be given to scientists, on the one hand, and also

artists, philosophers and intellectuals. In conclusion, the dichotomization of power appeared as a viable solution to the contradictions
of technocratic politics.

Technocratic ideas crossed the Atlantic in the twentieth century, thanks to Frederick Taylor. With Taylor, however, the
emphasis is less on political utopias and more on the organization
of production. Indeed, the main preoccupation in the USA at the
beginning of the century was the presence of widespread inefficiency
and systemic waste. Taylor advocated for the scientific method as
a solution to massive waste. Impressed with the development of
organization science and technology, he believed in the existence
of 'one best way' for each and every problem. The problem with
this statement, when translating it into public administration and
public policy, is that most policy puzzles are not amenable to 'one
best way'. Nobody really knows, for example, if there is an optimal
solution (from a technical point of view) to problems such as drugs,
poverty and crime. Nevertheless, the obsession with the 'one best
way' to be discovered by the rule of science was here to stay.

Intellectuals belonging to the Progressive movement took Taylor's
ideas into the analysis of the political system. They thought that
Taylorism had huge potential for the organization of public administration. Hence their insistence on scientific management in the
public sector. As Fischer, drawing upon Haber, observes, scientific
management, 'in addition to its techniques for engineering practical
reforms, served a powerful legitimating function. For profession-
ally oriented middle-class Progressives, the operational assumptions
of scientific management meshed smoothly with their basic values'
(Fischer 1990: 82). Briefly, scientific management became a concept including both efficiency and the values of 'hard work' and
'leadership by the competent'. In this case again, one of the main
components of the technocratic agenda was legitimacy. This ideological stance was strengthened by the argument that scientific management had potential for eliminating conflicts between the social
classes. Workers, managers and employers would respect and conform their behaviour to the laws of scientific management. Technocratic ideology, therefore, was advocated as a political anaesthetic
in a period of industrial strife and mass mobilization.

In the background of this scenario, a professional figure was
rising: the manager. Touraine among many others has clarified
that 'technocrats are not technicians but managers, whether they
belong to the administration of the state or to big businesses'

(Touraine 1974: 47–8). The technician has a narrow perspective, whilst the technocrat has a wider view: all in all, the technocrat is more a generalist and a coordinator of people and techniques than a specialized expert. In 1921, Thorstein Veblen drew attention to the fact that most of the managers were engineers. They, in his own words, 'make up the General Staff of the industrial system; and without their immediate and unremitting guidance and correction the industrial system will not work' (Veblen 1963: 82). According to Veblen, it is clear that the proper working of the industrial system is of paramount importance to the material welfare of a country. Hence the pivotal role of the economy. In turn, the economy depends on engineers, 'who alone are competent to manage it' (Veblen 1963: 83). Yet 'hitherto these men who so make up the general staff of the industrial system have not ... been vested with anything more than an occasional, haphazard, and tentative control of some disjointed sector of the industrial equipment' (Veblen 1963: 83). Quite correctly, Daniel Bell, in his introduction to the Harbinger edition of *The engineers and the price system* (Veblen 1963: 1–35), drew attention to Veblen's intellectual lineage: the separation of society into a productive class and an obsolete class comes directly from Saint-Simon. For Veblen the unproductive labour was that of industrialists and captains of finance. Other 'parasites' were to be found in professions not directly connected with production: for example, soldiers, lawyers and merchants.

Veblen dedicated a number of corrosive pages to how captains of industry and financiers produce waste instead of wealth. Essentially, they were blamed for their absentee ownership and, more importantly still, for creating what Veblen dubbed 'sabotage – something in the way or retardation, restriction, withdrawal, unemployment of plant and workmen – whereby production is kept short of productive capacity' (Veblen 1963: 42). In order to avoid over-production and maximize profits – his argument, certainly at odds with contemporary neoclassical economics, continued – the captains of industry have to generate a

> conscientious withdrawal of efficiency ... So the rate and volume of output must be adjusted to the needs of the market, not to the working capacity of the available resources, equipment and man power, nor to the community's need of consumable goods. Therefore there must always be a certain variable margin of unemployment of plant and man power. (Veblen 1963: 42–3)

Briefly, the systematic waste lamented by Taylor was explained by a Saint-Simonian dichotomization of society. Veblen did not like the market and capitalism. However, unlike his contemporary socialists, what he disliked most was not the exploitation of the people, but the waste of goods, that is, sabotage.[2]

The solution to this problem had to be radical and political. Veblen exhorted engineers to become class-conscious, to seize power – perhaps in the wake of the fatal collapse of capitalism – and to abolish the price system. Like Saint-Simon, he knew that legitimacy was the Achilles' heel of the technocratic project. He wrote in fact that the

> popular sentiment in this country will not tolerate the assumption of responsibility by the technicians, who are in the popular apprehension conceived to be a somewhat fantastic brotherhood of over-specialised cranks, not to be trusted out of sight except under the restraining hand of safe and sane business men.
>
> (Veblen 1963: 139–40)

It would be feasible to seize power through a general strike if only engineers achieved class-consciousness. More difficult would be to get legitimacy. Consequently, Veblen suggested accurate preparations, including a massive documentation of waste. Incidentally, it should be observed that Veblen perceived the different political problems raised by (a) the organization of engineers and the creation of class-consciousness; (b) the seize of power, epitomized by the dream of a 'Soviet of Technicians'; and (c) legitimacy and the maintenance of power. Although he did not conceptualize much on the third point, he was fully aware of its importance.

Veblen was instrumental in the emergence of a movement, appropriately called the Technocrats, which reached momentum in the USA between the Great Depression and the beginning of the New Deal. The story of this movement has been narrated magisterially by William Akin (1977): here it is sufficient to note that this movement reiterated Veblen's themes of waste and technocratic rescue. Howard Scott, one of the main leaders of this American movement, expressed his *Credo* with the following words (quoted by Fischer 1990: 85):

> In Technocracy we see science banishing waste, unemployment, hunger, and insecurity of income forever ... we see science replacing an economy of scarcity with an era of abundance ... [And] we see functional competence displacing grotesque and wasteful

incompetence, facts displacing disorder, industrial planning displacing industrial chaos.

As concerns the need to document waste, the Great Depression was the living proof of a technological economy unable to profit from its own resources. At the same time, the Technocrats equipped themselves with studies on energy resources in North America and tables illustrating how the economy was not running at its full potential. Indeed, their central thesis was that new technology had created the pre-conditions for the end of scarcity and for the begin-'ning of an era of abundance. However, society had failed to adjust to technological change. Society – the Technocrats argued – was still organized around the principle of production for profit and not production for use (Akin 1977: 65). The price system was no longer needed, yet it remained a central mechanism of regulation, thus creating inefficiency and waste. More precisely, the economic analysis of the Technocrats was based on four points. The first point was an act of faith, the argument that the problem of scarcity had disappeared thanks to technological development. People could afford to work two or three days a week, and only for twenty years, by fully exploiting the potential of modern technology. The second point was that the allocation of resources was regulated by monetary costs and the market. The problem with this system of regulation was that the 'distribution of goods was artificially limited by market and price considerations' (Akin 1977: 72). The third point – as explained by Akin – was that 'the price system vested power in the hands of businessmen, bankers, and financiers. These groups, knowing nothing but financial manipulation for profit, attempted to direct industry by non-technical methods' (Akin 1977: 73). The final point is that the captains of industry were profit maximizers. Contemporary economic theory would see no evil with this (quite the contrary indeed: the assumption of profit maximization is central to the efficient functioning of the market). But to technocrats it sounded like anathema. Profit maximization – they contended – does not yield efficiency, but waste.

This was the economic analysis of the technocrats. Where the project really failed, however, was in its political analysis. Technocracy did not become a mass political movement. One reason for this is that the New Deal offered a better and more democratic response to the Great Depression than technocracy. Akin (1977:

111) presents a second and more crucial reason: 'the Technocrats' failure to develop a viable political theory for achieving change was a more immediate factor in the movement's decline'. This thesis should be intended in two complementary senses. To begin with, the technocrats lacked a theory of political action: seizing power – as Veblen had observed – requires organization and mass political appeal. The Technocrats were obsessed with the problem of being ready with plans for the day of victory, and less interested in how to get to that day. Their organization was pestered with defections, internal squabbles and an endemic membership problem. In short, this was the deficiency of their *theory of action*. In addition, the movement suffered from an underdeveloped *political theory*. They were proud of being an 'apolitical movement' and never denied the undemocratic nature of the movement. However, this was not an asset, as they believed, but a liability, dubbed by Akin (1977: 165) 'the sterility of technical elitism'. He goes on to argue that:

> The Technocrats made a believable case for a kind of technological utopia, but their asking price was too high. The idea of political democracy still represented a stronger ideal than technical elitism. In the end, critics believed that the socially desirable goals that technology made possible could be achieved without the sacrifice of existing institutions and values. (Akin 1977: 150)

In conclusion, the Technocrats' project was too sterile to become a convincing political justification for the 'rule by experts'. For the first time in history, technocracy changed from a political utopia into a movement with a precise political goal, seizing power. However, political ideology and deeply rooted legitimacy are indispensable pre-conditions for words to become action and change the world. The failure of the Technocrats sheds light on the vital relationship between expertise and legitimacy: functional legitimacy (that is, competence as the legitimacy base for playing key functions in the economy) does not translate automatically into political legitimacy (that is, the legitimacy to play political functions).

James Burnham, in his *The managerial revolution* (1941) drew attention to a drawback in the analysis of the Technocrats. He argued that they had stressed the role of engineers and technical experts, thus neglecting the role of managers. In actuality, it was managers (production managers, administrative engineers, and supervisory technicians) who had *de facto* control of the economy:

direction and coordination had become more important than technical tasks. The point, as already mentioned, will be confirmed by subsequent studies (Touraine 1974) and illustrates an ambiguity of technocratic analysis. This ambiguity is related to the different empirical referents (in terms of professions or classes) of scholars of technocratic power. Later on we will turn to this point again. Now it is useful to stress that Burnham's analysis had two political implications. First, he noticed that the state had become a key player in the economy. The smooth functioning of the economy required massive state intervention. In turn this implied planning and a large bureaucratic apparatus. The 'new class' of managers was assuming power both in the private sector and in public administration. Second, the obsolescence of capitalism – he contended – had blurred the divide between capitalism and socialism. Indeed, he argued for a systematic structural convergence of capitalism and socialism. Both systems were converging towards the managerial society.

After World War Two the theme of convergence was at the centre of the debate in the 1960s, fuelled by the idea of the 'end of ideology'. The spread of technical decision making had undermined ideology, argued Daniel Bell in his book on *The end of ideology* (Bell 1960). Galbraith contributed to the debate on convergence by arguing that market imperatives and profit maximization were being substituted by planning, the management of aggregate demand, and the stabilization of the price system. Companies – in his opinion – were ruled by collective decisions informed by expertise, not by the 'animal spirits' of entrepreneurial individuals. Further, the state was a pivotal actor in the economy for two reasons. Not only was the state deeply engaged in the stabilization of the economy via the management of aggregate demand, it was also involved in assuring the expansion of higher education, essential to long-term economic growth. Thus the state was evolving from the traditional liberal state of the previous century into a 'new industrial state'.

However, according to Galbraith, an exclusive emphasis on managers was inadequate. 'Management' – he wrote – 'is a collective and imperfectly defined entity . . . It includes . . . only a small proportion of those who, as participants, contribute information to group decisions' (Galbraith 1967: 71). The group of people who ensured the rise of the modern corporation is defined in the much-quoted passage on the technostructure. This group:

Is very large; it extends from the most senior officials of the corporation to where it meets, at the outer perimeter, the white and blue
collar workers whose function is to conform more or less mechanic-
ally to instruction or routine. It embraces all who bring specialised
knowledge, talent or experience to group decision-making. This,
not the management, is the guiding intelligence – the brain – of the
enterprise. There is no name for all who participate in group decision-
making or the organisation which they form. I propose to call this
organisation the Technostructure.   (Galbraith 1967: 71)

What are the political implications of this analysis? Like other
authors, Galbraith has shed light on the tension between expertise
and democracy. Who will make the technostructure responsive to
the people? For Galbraith the solution is in the educational system.
Not only are the institutions of higher education a fundamental
resource of the complex modern economy, they are also the loci
of enlightened debate, critical reflection, pluralism and healthy
scepticism. Within the political arena, the technostructure would
be tamed and guided by the education system. *Mutatis mutandis*,
Galbraith, like Comte and Saint-Simon, has turned to the medieval
distinction between temporal and spiritual power. The problem
with this analysis is that the primacy of the educated spirits is
more evoked than investigated. In the end, mere wishful thinking
for the future.

The debate on the political consequences of a society dominated by expertise has polarized around the extremes of optimistic
and pessimistic views of the future. Indeed, the interest in the
future is a characteristic of this literature. Of course, the strategy
of looking at the future has its own problems, most crucially
perhaps the fact that expectations have a premium over systematic
analysis. Like Galbraith, Daniel Bell, the prophet of the post-
industrial society (Bell 1973) is not pessimistic. The thrust of Bell's
analysis is that the post-industrial society, notwithstanding its limitations, is inherently 'meritocratic'. This yields a ray of hope for
social justice. Ferkiss holds a deep faith in the virtues of his *Technological man* (1969). The subtitle of his book is *the myth and the
reality*, but, paradoxically, his vision of the new politics in the
technological era is almost mythological. Thanks to technology,
people would be in control of their destiny. This will pave the way
to a rediscovery of politics, centred on a philosophy of new natural-
ism, holism and immanism (Williams 1971: 42). In stark opposition,
Ellul (1965) is literally terrified by technocratic governance. In his

view, technical determinism, planning and a state power enhanced by propaganda and political psychology will turn the world into a place of apathy and sheer domination.

Finally, and more recently, a group of authors (reviewed by Burris 1993 and Fischer 1990), the so-called 'new class theorists', have seen in the educated workers a new revolutionary actor. While previous studies expressed worries about the anti-democratic tendencies of technocrats, this group of authors argues that the new class has been socialized into the values of creativity, open discourse, free communication, and autonomy. In turn, these beliefs and attitudes clash with the imperatives of bureaucratized structures dominating the company and the state. The new class, therefore, has as much antagonistic potential as the proletariat. Alvin Gouldner (1979), however, has contended that the new class is both emancipatory and elitist. On the one hand, the new class is for emancipation and open communication. On the other, it sets itself in a privileged position by claiming that its knowledge is better, more reflexive and insightful than alternative forms of knowledge. Additionally, as observed by Burris, 'one political issue that has not received enough attention concerns the relationship between the New Class of technical experts and more traditional élites, such as capitalist owners, corporate managers, and political leaders' (Burris 1993: 43). This is a key – yet unexplored – issue for technocratic theory. Fischer is one of the few authors who has reflected upon this issue. We will turn in a moment to his ideas on the 'politics of expertise', but the essential argument is that traditional elites and technocrats tend to coalesce: a 'close alliance' – he argues – 'holds out the potential for a mutually beneficial strategy' (Fischer 1990: 112). This alliance is a new system of elite politics, with the following characteristics:

> Grounded in technical competence of professional expertise, such a system, not only shrouds critical decisions in what would appear to be the logic of technical imperatives, it also erects stringent barriers to popular participation. Only those with knowledge (or credentials) can hope to participate in deciding the sophisticated issues confronting post-industrial society.   (Fischer 1990: 112)

Putnam, in his study of political elites in Germany, Italy and the UK, found a new hybrid, the 'politician-technician' (Putnam 1976; 1977). This, as Fischer himself argues, appears to corroborate the hypothesis of a close alliance. However, more systematic work, particularly on public policy making, is certainly needed before the delicate issue of the relationship between experts and politicians can be tackled with success.

An assessment of technocratic theory

The literature on technocracy provides useful insights into the politics of expertise, but its limitations are manifold. In this section I set out to first review the contribution of the studies examined above and then to discuss their limitations. Fischer (1990) has underlined the main difference between the earlier stage of technocratic utopias and the contemporary technocrat. The former advocated for a direct rise to power of experts, whereas the latter is formally respectful of democratic values and institutions. Nobody is currently arguing for a government of scientists, nor has it been maintained that the formal institutions of democracy should be turned into Soviets of Technicians *à la* Veblen. But technocrats are gaining power informally, in the shadow of formal structures: advisory boards (Boston 1988), think tanks (Fischer 1993; Stone *et al.* 1998), regulatory agencies (Majone 1996; Shapiro 1997) and governments teeming with non-elected ministers are the primary loci where experts have now secured a pivotal position.

Moreover, social sciences – and particularly public choice, cost-benefit analysis, and a certain use of the tools of public policy analysis – have now gained good currency in public administration and, more generally, public decision making. Hence the technocratic challenge is not confined to the engineers, but involves the policy sciences too (Lerner and Lasswell 1956; Lindblom 1990).[3]

Turning to the politics of expertise, the point to emphasize is the *change in the nature of power*. This change has the following components. First, knowledge and expertise become the terrain of politics (Fischer 1990). A corollary of this can be the direct involvement of technocrats in politics. Even though many policy experts (especially administrative elites trained in the natural sciences and technology: see Putnam 1977) are still sceptical towards political participation, there has been also a politicization of expertise. The case of right-wing think tanks in countries such as Australia, the US and the UK is indicative of this politicization (Stone *et al.* 1998). If some experts still prefer the option of professing political alienation, there is also evidence of social and natural scientists entering the political fray without the mask of neutrality. Either way, sophisticated expertise remains a key political resource in the policy process. The second component of the change in the nature of power refers to the depoliticization of the public sphere (Fischer 1990). Due to its complexity, public policy is often insulated from public debate and pressure from below. The debate on the level of interest rate, for example, is confined to monetary policy experts, although the conduct of monetary policy has important implications for the ordinary citizen. This opacity of public policy is therefore a second important characteristic of power change. Social movements, diffuse interests, and public opinion are silenced in that they are deprived of their voice in public policy. They may even be accused of being incompatible with the complexities and the functional needs of contemporary government. According to some forms of technocratic discourse, political participation creates 'overload', triggers 'zero-sum games', and produces stalemate in situations where technical decision making could instead find the 'best' solution efficiently.[4] Accordingly, technocrats should preside over a depoliticized public sphere.

The change in the nature of power is accompanied by the rise of the *technocratic mentality* within administrative elites. Putnam (1976) shows that the technocrat is fundamentally hostile to the openness of democracy, and suspicious of parliamentary institutions (see also Meynaud 1969). Political conflict is not considered a healthy component of democracy, but a consequence of ignorance. Rational analysis and knowledge produce efficient solutions that should be accepted by all people of good will. Hence 'the technocrat believes that social and political conflict is often, at best, misguided, and, at worst, contrived' (Putnam 1977: 386). A corollary is that the technocratic mentality is more concerned with technological progress, efficiency and material productivity than with fairness and social justice (Putnam 1977: 387).

As already hinted, technocracy is based on the construction of *legitimacy*. The ideological dimension of technocracy should not be forgotten. Technocrats seek legitimacy by arguing for 'the government of science'. The reality is – as Sartori (1987) observes – that 'government by reason' always means 'government of scientists'. 'Governments will always be of persons, never of things. Hence, there is little doubt as to who will be the king: if a government of science were ever to exist, it would be a government of scientists' (Sartori 1987: 438). Another fundamental ideological component of technocracy is the *Credo* of the primacy of competence in a complex society. Competence yields both functional legitimacy (expertise is needed in certain key functions) and a connotation of social justice (rewarding competence with political power is part and parcel of meritocracy). At the same time, technocratic ideology plays down the role of traditional politics. The latter is pictured as a world of corruption, chaos, self-interested politicians, and inefficiency. Indeed, technocracy desperately needs mass apathy. It proliferates when public participation is reduced to a minimum and the *res publica* becomes professionalized.

Turning to the limitations, I argue that technocratic theory is flawed because of (a) its emphasis; (b) its conceptual limitations; (c) its empirical imprecision; and (d) considerations of political theory. The problem with emphasis is that most of the literature is ideological, predictive, prescriptive, and on occasion fatalistic. The actual making of public policy is not systematically investigated. Technocratic theory tends to prefer broad characterizations of society and politics. As a consequence, it does not provide information on when and how knowledge becomes political power. Social classes, the organization of the workplace and the economy are the main subjects of analyses of technocracy. However, the state receives less consideration. This is a serious limitation of emphasis: because of this, the literature has not answered the question whether the state has changed its very nature in post-industrial societies (see also Williams 1971: 10).

The conceptual limitations are not less serious, especially in terms of ambiguities. To begin with, different authors refer to different key professional figures when they talk about technocracy. Who are the technocrats? Engineers, managers, the technostructure, social scientists working in government and within think tanks? There is a wide gamut of professions who have been from time to time considered as the quintessence of technocracy. The reader of the literature, as a consequence, is puzzled with this dispersion. To make things worse, the literature does not clarify the question whether the technocrats are a social class or a profession. If they are a social class their political identity should be stronger than if they are just professionals. Class-consciousness makes a difference in politics. Finally, a conceptual limitation arises out of the fact that the difference between getting power and maintaining-exerting power is overlooked. Both in Latin America and in Europe, academics have been significantly empowered due to the profound crisis of traditional political structures, and particularly political parties. Thanks to their competence and (perceived) neutrality, experts drawn from the academic world seized direct political power in a number of countries. Competence and distance from the world of 'dirty politics' were essential resources of legitimate authority. Nevertheless, these professors in government have not maintained their power in government by means of scientific rationality (whatever that means) but through traditional politics. The problems of consensus, coalitions, and ultimately political power were not converted *ipso facto* into a rational exercise. Experts have to behave *politically* if they do not want to lose power, although they can draw upon a stock of legitimacy fuelled by competence. Political power – as noted by Domenico Fisichella (1997), a political scientist who became nothing less than vice-president of the Italian Senate – does not evaporate with the 'rule by experts': it changes, but does not fade away!

Technocratic theory, in general, is also poor in empirical analysis. As averred, it does not provide a great deal of information on the state, on public policy making and on how knowledge enters the policy process. If one compares this literature with the results of systematic studies of public policy making the difference is immense. Authors who have investigated how public policy is made have collected more empirical evidence on the failures of technocratic policy making than on its successes. Studies on knowledge utilization have shown that knowledge enters the policy process in combination with power and interests, thus becoming intrinsically political, that decisions are the result of multiple actors struggling with limited rationality, and that the 'heroic' model of science directing choice in public policy without political interference is not corroborated by empirical evidence (Collingridge and Reeve 1986; Radaelli 1995; Weiss 1979; Wittrock 1982).[5] The policy process is not so linear and simplistic as technocratic theory claims: hierarchy and planning, two common themes of technocratic literature, often do not play a large role, especially when policy is the product of networks of interaction (Rhodes 1997). No competence or superior techniques have already taken the place of social interaction. Barker and Peters (1992) make an additional critical point when they observe that, empirically, competition and conflict exist within science. For example, there is public competition for money and for attention from the mass media. Rudig, and with him a plethora of empirical studies on nuclear power and environmental controversies, notes that 'scientists have engaged as important critics of technology, expressing dissent in the public domain and lending their support to protest movements opposing particular technological developments' (Rudig 1992: 17–18). Of course, there are many more scientists defending technology, but the point here is that apoliticized technocratic direction of public policy is not common.

Finally, there are the limitations highlighted by public policy analysis (Lindblom 1959; 1990) and political theory (Dahl 1985; Habermas 1970; 1971). One common assumption of technocratic ideology is the reification of the common good. In order to play a powerful political role, there must be such a thing as the 'best way' (Taylor) or the 'best technical answer' to the puzzles raised by collective problems. The assumption holds true only in what Lindblom has dubbed synoptic decision making. In actuality, the common good is what multiple actors discover through social interaction and learning, in a word by dint of their involvement in the policy process (Lindblom 1990). Political decisions, moreover, are all about values and beliefs, they are not a simple matter of empirical statements (Dahl 1985). Further, Habermas has argued that rationality has two dimensions. There is the practical-instrumental dimension of rationality, but there is also the expressive and normative dimension. Both have their place in politics, both are necessary to the process of knowing (Habermas 1971). The *reductio ad unum* of technocracy, therefore, is unacceptable: to reiterate, instrumental rationality is only one component of politics.

In conclusion, the literature on technocracy is only a point of departure (and not a terribly good one) for the analysis of the policy process. Recent studies on the politics of expertise and knowledge utilization detect the presence of typical technocratic themes, but within a new political context (such as the crisis of political parties, the increasing complexity of public policy, the overt political role of think tanks, and new forms of technocratic legitimacy). The analysis of the EU policy process should proceed more from the insights provided by this recent literature than from standard technocratic theory. The political peculiarities of the EU suggest, in any case, a closer examination of the making of public policy in Brussels. This will be the major theme in the next chapter.

Notes

1 Following Fisichella, I would like to add the name of the Sicilian baron Giuseppe Corvaja who wrote a *Catechismo Bancocratico* (Bancocratic catechism, 1841) which fits in nicely with the *Catéchisme des Industriels* by Saint-Simon (1823–24) and the *Catéchisme Positiviste* by Comte (1852). The Sicilian gentleman's book could perhaps be seen as a prophecy of the extraordinary power enjoyed by central bankers in the contemporary economy, but it should not be forgotten that the fascination with bankers was a common literary theme in the nineteenth century, as epitomized by the works of de Balzac and Stendhal (Fisichella 1997: 5).

2 See Adorno (1941), quoted by Bell in his introduction to Veblen (1963: 33).

3 However, it should be noted that the tools of public policy are not inherently technocratic. To mention an important example, policy evaluation is often blamed for being the perfect tool of technocratic management (Fischer 1990). The reality is that it all depends on *how* policy evaluation is employed. More precisely, at stake is the conceptualization of the policy process (Radaelli and Dente 1996). If the policy process is reduced to a rational-synoptic process, then policy evaluation and similar policy instruments acquire a technocratic bias. By contrast, policy evaluation can play a role of enlightenment and learning if public policy is conceptualized as the result of a diffuse decision-making process, where multiple actors with limited rationality seek to make sense of collective problems (Lindblom 1959; 1990).

4 For a classic analysis of government overload see Crozier *et al.* (1975). The idea of a zero-sum society appeared first in Thurow (1981).

5 Consider also the disillusionment of US social scientists engaged in the Great Society under President Johnson (Aaron 1978) and in later policy reforms (Aaron 1989).

CHAPTER THREE

Technocracy and European Union public policy making

It is now time we turned to the EU when assessing the intellectual potential of technocratic theory. What are we to make of the literature on technocracy, thinking of the EU? This literature provides useful insights on the politics of expertise, the changing nature of politics, and the depoliticization of the public sphere. EU policies are technical and relatively opaque. Consequently, there is scope for probing these ideas, provided that EU policy making is fleshed out in more detail. This is the purpose of this chapter. The illustration of the technocratic legacy of the past will introduce the examination of the EU as a political system specialized in the production of regulatory policy. An examination of the policy process, however, requires identification of the main actors and of the political mechanisms shaping the process itself. For this reason, a number of actor-based models of the policy-making process will be reviewed, before a description of an important mechanism of technocratic legitimacy (that is, policy transfer) is presented. A general assessment of technocracy versus other models of the EU policy process will conclude the chapter.

The original conception and its legacy

Scholars of organizational behaviour have shown how the stage of initial formation affects the development of organizations (Eliassen and Svaasand 1975). The early traits of an organization, the way the structure of power takes shape at the beginning, the main dimensions of organizational institutionalization are 'congealed' and this imprinting marks further development. A corollary of this proposition is that in order to understand an organization's present, one has to trace its past and look for elements of organizational power providing continuity. The European institutions have remained strikingly similar to those designed by Jean Monnet[1] and the other founding fathers of the European Coal and Steel Community (ECSC, established in 1951) and the European Economic Community (1957).[2] This is why it is of great importance to examine the origins of European integration.

The early stage of European integration was marked by a technocratic approach embodied in the Monnet Plan for the ECSC (Featherstone 1994; Heyen 1992).[3] The key idea of the plan was the special position given to experts in the making of supranational public policy. Hence the idea of a High Authority composed of selected experts.[4] Those experts, however, were not to operate in isolation from the society. The Monnet method of integration prefigured a system of *engrenage* whereby networks of interest groups, organized labour and firms affected by European public policy would be gradually involved in the making of public policy (Haas 1958). The founding fathers of European integration envisaged governance by technocratic consensus. The engine of integration would be represented by a combination of technocrats and interest groups, building together supranational coalitions in favour of European public policy (Haas 1958). Wallace and Smith (1995: 140) point out that the ordinary citizen was absolutely neglected in this approach:

> Monnet strategy was of élite-led gradualism, with the expectation that popular consent would slowly follow that lead. In such an indirect approach to political integration, the locking in of interested organisations – from business, labour, and from national administrative agencies – was a much higher priority than the direct involvement of as yet uninformed public.

As Featherstone puts it, this was a process of 'élite capture: the ability of the EC Commission to engage key economic élites and to help them recognise their self-interest in supporting greater unity' (Featherstone 1994: 155). The method envisaged for the ECSC was to be revisited yet again in the Treaty of Rome (1957). Wallace and Smith observe that 'enlightened administration on behalf of uninformed publics, in cooperation with affected interests and subject to the approval of national governments, was therefore the compromise again struck in the Treaties of Rome' (Wallace and Smith 1995: 143).

An important characteristic of this method was incrementalism. Integration would proceed initially by limited policy domains, such as steel and coal, and later 'spill-over' to other policies. Thus the original conception of the European Community contemplated two technocratic aspects. One was the step by step approach, based on sound economic arguments and incontestable gains to achieve by means of integration. In other words, this meant hiding the political content of integration behind the smoke-screen of limited economic decisions. Another was the pivotal role of experts. Monnet had not even conceived of a Council of Ministers, presumably because the High Authority had a limited competence, confined to steel and coal policy. But this is also indicative of his technocratic approach. It was up to the Belgian and Dutch delegations to raise the point of a Council to counterbalance the High Authority and provide political direction. This neglect of politics has survived throughout the years, as illustrated by Featherstone (1994: 159 and 161):

> the power of the High Authority and the Commission differed, but much of the philosophy underpinning the role of today's Commission stems directly from Monnet's conception of the High Authority ... Fundamental to Monnet's beliefs was the need to tie governments to the European objectives, but to have them entrust much of the task for their attainment to the technocratic High Authority, a body which he thought should be barely accountable to them.

The model chosen for the European Economic Community was also original in that it was not a mere imitation of models already in place in one or more of the six founding countries. True, in very general terms the High Authority (and later the Commission) resembled the French administration for its technocratic characteristics.[5] But the Commission offers a good example of innovations with no direct precedents. As shown by Cassese and della Cananea (1992: 93), the Commissioners are neither diplomats nor politicians. Rather, they are hybrids in that they share some characteristics with diplomats and politicians, but bound to act as repositories of the Community's interest. A Commissioner, although nominated by a national government, is somewhat isolated from political pressures and, unlike diplomats, does not have to respect the foreign policy goals of that government. Moreover – Cassese and della Cananea (1992: 93) observe – 'the absence of a clear distinction between legislative and administrative acts and activities did not derive from the member states' tradition'. The Commission is not a mere executing body, has the power to propose legislation, and intervenes directly in implementing competition policy.

It would be utterly wrong to imagine that Monnet had envisaged a large 'technostructure', to paraphrase Galbraith (see Chapter Two), in charge of European public policy making. Instead, Monnet argued for a small group of highly-skilled dedicated people independent from national governments, prepared to take decisions in a collegiate fashion, and loyal to the European spirit. These people were to operate in a very small non-hierarchical structure (Mazey 1992: 33; Monnet 1978: 373). However, as Mazey shows in her analysis of the bureaucratization of the High Authority, 'within the period of four years the administrative services of the High Authority were transformed from an informal grouping of sympathetic individuals into a professional bureaucracy, which, in terms of its structure and "technocratic" character, resembled the French administration' (Mazey 1992: 43). The adoption of the French model was not without its consequences as France is the European country where technocratic tendencies in the policy process have been most pronounced (Dyson 1980). Hierarchy is one of the features of the original model, which has remained more or less intact in the passage from the High Authority to the Commission. Even recently, a systematic analysis of the Commission has described it as 'rigid, very hierarchic, fragmented, compartmentalised in complex ways, sometimes incoherent' (Stevens and Stevens 1996: 11). The original model, therefore, has remained congealed within the organization, exactly as hypothezised by organizational theory.

The politics of regulation

The technocratic legacy is not confined to the Commission, but pervades the whole political structure of the EU. A comprehensive analysis has argued that the EU is based on three mechanisms of representation (Andersen and Burns 1996: 230): expert representation ('in the context of a stress on "rationality" and effectiveness' – Andersen and Burns clarify), representation of interest groups (and diffuse interests) in policy networks, and national representation (this refers to the constant presence of member states' representatives in the EU policy process). However, parliamentary-territorial representation is less developed, as illustrated by the hyphenated line in Figure 3.1.

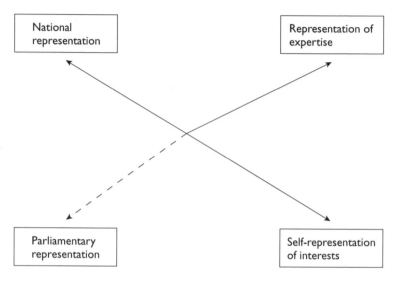

Figure 3.1 *Forms of representation in the European Union*
Source: This figure stems from the analysis conducted by Andersen and Burns (1996)

European Union governance is based on the direct participation of affected interests (domestic interests, business preferences, and diffuse demands) in policy networks. The level of expertise necessary to participate in EU public policy making does not make it amenable to traditional parliamentary oversight. Hence 'expert sovereignty tends to prevail over popular sovereignty or parliamentary sovereignty' (Andersen and Burns 1996: 229).

Andersen and Burns point out that the EU policy process is focused on efficiency. This emphasis is associated with the specialization of the EU as a political system producing regulatory policy.[6] In this respect, the EU has developed differently than nation-states. The EU in fact does not, and probably will not, follow the typical trajectories of political development of the nation-states, as we have known them in Western Europe. Not only is there (by comparison with the nation-state) a discontinuity in terms of institutional development (parliament, government and bureaucracy radically change form and substance as we move from national to Union level), but specialization in terms of types of public policies is very different too. While the nation-states developed and consolidated around distributive and redistributive policies (in brief, welfare and taxation policies), the EU – as Gian Domenico Majone's studies have shown – has chiefly developed the regulatory dimension.

One can explain the growth of regulation at the European level in various ways. Following Majone (1996), for instance, one can argue in terms of demand and supply. On the demand front, European firms often consider with favour the adoption of one single European rule instead of fifteen, so as to be able to speak to the rest of the world with a single voice. For the member states, the Union's regulatory policies are a response to those problems that cannot be solved by mere intergovernmental agreements.

Credibility is another important factor in the demand side of EU regulation (Majone 1996). In an integrated economic area, rules are an important resource of regulatory competition (Egan 1998: 488; Majone 1996). Countries seek to make their firms more competitive by relaxing rules, even when this leads to market failures. There are good political reasons for doing this. Governments are sensitive to the electoral cycle: a politician in office may prefer not to impose too many regulatory requirements on citizens and firms. The credibility of national regulators is therefore the Achilles' heel of domestic regulatory regimes. This credibility dilemma can be solved by delegating rule-making power to European institutions. Institutions such as the Commission are in a better position. Not only is the Commission less politically and physically 'close' than national governments to companies in various countries, but, most crucially, given its bureaucratic nature, it is not sensitive to electoral cycles and inter-party competition. When regulation is politically expensive for governments and credibility of domestic regimes is low, delegation of regulatory powers to supranational institutions represents the most viable solution.[7]

A further factor is that the costs of European regulation are not undergone in the first instance by the governments. Indeed, firms and citizens have to pay the costs of adapting to a directive, let us say, on pesticides, or toy manufacture, or safety belts. This factor should be borne in mind, since it is representatives of national governments that sit on the Council. At the Council level, political agreement is easier where, in the first instance,[8] firms and citizens pay adjustment costs. The proof is that in sectors where costs are paid directly by states (as with the abolition of double taxation on company profits, a measure that directly hits national revenues), Europeanization has been very limited (as illustrated in Chapter Five).[9]

Continuing with the metaphor of demand for and supply of regulation, the Commission, as explained by Majone (1996), is in a formidable position for the supply of regulation. The EU budget constraint bars the development of distributive and redistributive policies (since social policy programmes require large sums of money), but to write a rule that, say, lays down requirements for engaging in credit or for international mergers and acquisitions, the only resource needed is a thorough knowledge of the markets and the subjects to be regulated. The Commission is, without a shadow of doubt, a bureaucracy wherein cognitive resources are most developed.

As far as the relationship with the regulated subjects is concerned, the very numerous working groups that meet every day at the Commission have extended the network of interactions. In his writings, Majone refers to the idea of *copinage technocratique* to denote an intense system of interaction between Brussels officials, experts from industry, and national civil servants. Thus the original system of *engrenage* envisaged by Monnet still plays its main function of providing relatively smooth policy making within circles of experts.

The Commission, moreover, like all bureaucracies, is oriented towards expanding its own powers (Majone 1996). The mission to promote and deepen European integration is even laid down in the Treaties, and this is what is referred to when the Commission is spoken of as the 'engine of integration'. Analysts of European public policies, finally, have highlighted the Commission's role as policy entrepreneur, a term designating a political subject capable of opportunistically exploiting the scarce resources at its own disposal in order to create new policies.[10]

Further, the growth of regulation – apart from the points raised by Majone – can also result from a manifest political asymmetry of the European political system.[11] At the national level, a minister of the environment willing to propose environmental policy rules has to deal, inside the government, with his or her colleagues for industry, commerce and agriculture. These colleagues will assert the needs not to put too heavy a burden on companies, shops and farmers. Other colleagues in the treasury will preside over the economic compatibility of the proposals and therefore will press the minister proposing new environmental rules with requests for cost-benefit analysis. At the national level, then, there is a political mechanism – the collegiate action of government – that brings a plurality of interests inside the policy formation process. If, however, the hypothetical environment minister decided to operate at the European level, he or she would have to convince only his or her environment ministers from the other member states. It is certainly true that the proposals would have to come from the Commission, which seeks, operating in collegiate fashion, to weigh the various demands and interests, but at the Environment Council it is only the environmental ministers who are in charge of the final decision. This asymmetry leads to a systematic bias towards the growth of regulation.

It is beyond the scope of this book to assess the implications of the politics of regulation for the theory of the EU (see however Caporaso 1996). Here it is sufficient to observe that the EU is a political system with a comparative advantage in the production of regulation. Knowledge, rather than budget, is the critical resource in regulatory policy making, and the Commission utilizes this resource extensively. Regulatory policies aim at efficiency, rather than redistribution. This makes them suitable for discussion and for negotiations in expert circles, whereas redistribution kindles the passions of politicians, political parties and the mass opinion because of its impact on the class structure. Efficiency is a positive-sum game, where nobody is worse off. Redistribution, instead, implies that resources are taken from a portion of the society and allocated to another. The emphasis on efficiency and positive-sum games is consistent with the essential thrust of the technocratic mentality (Meynaud 1969; Putnam 1977). The technocrat believes that rational analysis and scientific examination of facts will bring about unanimous consensus on policy solutions. By contrast, the technocrat feels uneasy under conditions of political conflict, ideological debates, and controversies on distributive issues of social justice.

Concluding on this point, the politics of regulation in the EU is consistent with the technocratic legacy of the original model. In its current form, regulation is the type of policy that suits better the expertise of the Commission, the tendency towards technical negotiation and the general avoidance of open political debate. A scholar of US regulatory policies concluded his comprehensive analysis by stating that 'What we have, for the most part, then, is government by experts ... The goal of such experts is not responsiveness or social justice but rather administrative efficiency, or scientific rigour' (Gormley 1985–86: 619). Gormley analysed regulation in a mature democracy (the USA) with a considerable experience of democratic control and political oversight over regulatory bodies. He had to conclude that regulatory policy was turning into government by experts.[12] What about the EU, whose democracy and legitimacy are still vigorously questioned? Has it turned into an ideal regulatory environment for technocracy? Regulation is an important element of the structure of the EU as a political system. But a more in-depth investigation of the policy-making process is needed at this point. It is to this topic that we now turn.

Actors in the EU policy process: bureaucratic politics, epistemic communities and advocacy coalitions

A significant characteristic of the making of European public policy is the presence of bureaucratic politics. This term was originally introduced by Allison (with an emphasis on international relations) and Downs (with an emphasis on domestic politics) and has been applied to the EU by Peters.[13] Bureaucratic politics – as originally fleshed out by Allison and Downs – posits that the units of a governmental apparatus are quasi-autonomous actors with their own purposive and reflexive goals.[14] In the case of the EU, bureaucratic politics takes two forms, namely *bureaucratic competition* between (and even within) institutions and the organization of the policy process around functional policy areas (*fragmented public policy making*). Bureaucratic competition involves European institutions such as the Commission, the Council, and the European Parliament. In this process, for example, the Commission will seek to expand its power *vis-à-vis* other EU institutions. Not only does competition for power place one institution of the EU against another, but also even within the same institution there can be an intense turf battle. Studies of the Commission offer a picture of Directorate Generals with different administrative cultures (Cini 1996) and diverse policy frameworks (Harcourt 1998). For example, DG IV has developed its own culture of competition policy and tends to see policy issues through the lenses of the competition approach (or 'framework', see Harcourt 1998). By contrast, DG XV – the single market Directorate – is the most ardent supporter of a single market approach to policy issues. When new issues crop up on the Commission's agenda, DG XV tends to argue that they should be processed by relying on the single market approach. Different approaches and alternative administrative cultures within the Commission imply that on the same issue there will be a fight over who controls the agenda and how should an issue be defined. Under these circumstances, bureaucratic politics filters into the Commission itself, with the DGs and their respective Commissioners pitched one against the other. Media ownership policy (Chapter Six) will provide a paradigmatic case of bureaucratic politics within the Commission.

The second level of bureaucratic politics sheds further light on the EU policy process. This is the level of specific policy areas. Essentially, policy making is organized around a certain number of functional policy areas where Directorates of the Commission, Commissioners, committees of the European Parliament, Council's advisory groups, national administrations and interest groups form coalitions vying for power (Peters 1992: 116; Richardson 1996). Fragmentation, coalition formation, bargaining, networking and intense negotiation in sectorial arenas are the features of this level of bureaucratic politics.

It should be added that the EU political system presents multiple points of access (Peters 1994). There is no central coordinating actor, such as a central government. There are no majorities giving birth, after elections, to a government with a legislative mandate to be implemented. And the role of political parties in controlling the public agenda is extraordinarily limited when compared to their role in domestic political systems. In this sense, the EU policy process can be described as decentralized. As Peters explains 'whether or not the bureaucracy, either European or national, is the dominant player (and it often is), the policy-making process has the characteristics of decentralisation and local control typical of the bureaucratic form of policy-making' (Peters 1992: 118).

The dominance of fragmented, 'pillarized' politics in the EU has important consequences. One is that the making of policies becomes insulated from macro-political scrutiny, public oversight, and governmental control. Another is the intense competition for power (as opposed to learning and more cooperative problem-solving styles) in the policy process. Political competition in a system with multiple points of access will make it difficult to produce coherent and efficient policy, however. As Peters comments, 'institutionally, the actors will strive to preserve their own powers, perhaps even if it means reducing the capacity of the resulting arrangements to make "good" policy for the Community as a whole' (Peters 1992: 118).

'Insulated', sectorial, technical policy making is a particularly appropriate precondition for the type of 'apolitical' policy making described by the technocratic literature. Coalitions including administrative officials (at the EU and national levels) and pressure groups can be seen as the modern version of the system of *engrenage* built into the original model of the Community by Jean Monnet. The presence of multiple points of access in the EU political system is yet another reason for doubting the possibility to exercise political oversight on EU public policy formation. This is a prima facie indicator of technocratic policy making in the EU, although I will try to be more precise on the use of the terms 'bureaucratic politics' and 'technocracy' in the conclusive section of this chapter.

However, in certain circumstances the main issue at stake is not the competition for power among institutions 'striving to preserve their own power', as Peters puts it. EU policies often touch upon areas of great uncertainty. Environmental policy or genetic manipulation are good examples of areas of EU policy where the dominant theme is radical uncertainty. Of course, the competition for power and reflexive goals is still at stake when the environmental committee of the European Parliament, for example, presses the Council on a directive concerning the quality of water. But under conditions of uncertainty policy making is also 'puzzling', not mere 'powering' (Heclo 1974). This consideration draws our attention to the political role of communities of experts (for example, scientists with political power) in the EU.

Faced with the increasing role of scientific arguments and genuine uncertainty, a nascent body of literature has identified the presence of 'epistemic communities' in the EU (Radaelli 1997; Richardson 1996; Verdun 1997; Zito 1998). Originally, Peter Haas developed the concept of 'epistemic community' for the understanding of international policy coordination. The concept has the aim of 'turning the study of political process into a question about who learns what, when, to whose benefit, and why' (Adler and Haas 1992: 370). The emphasis should be placed on 'learning' because under conditions of radical uncertainty learning becomes a fundamental mechanism of policy development.

The term epistemic community defines 'a network of professionals with recognised expertise and competence in a particular domain and an authoritative claim to policy-relevant knowledge' within that domain or issue-area (Haas 1992: 3). The epistemic community approach introduces three characteristics of the policy process: uncertainty, interpretation and institutionalization of ideas. When there is uncertainty – Haas argues – there is not a clear perception of what the interest of the actor is: accordingly, an epistemic community is able to generate a definition of interests by illuminating certain dimensions of an issue, from which an actor can deduce her/his interests. Interests therefore become a dynamic dependent variable, framed by knowledge. Thus – Haas argues – 'many of the conditions facilitating a focus on power are absent. It is difficult for leaders to identify their potential political allies. Neither power nor institutional cues to behaviour will be available, and new patterns of action may ensue' (Haas 1992: 14). Uncertainty implies that actors puzzle over public policy. Actors offering interpretation are in a pivotal position because policy is first and foremost an attempt to understand and decode a complex reality. Interestingly, Muller has defined public policy as 'the construction of a relationship with the world' and has noted the political analogy between *prise de parole* (production of meaning) and *prise de pouvoir*, or the structuration of power relations (Muller 1995: 164). Put differently, the production of meaning is the key to the definition of interests and to the institutionalization of policy ideas.[15]

Epistemic communities have power only when they are organically inserted into the policy process. Their role is constrained: often epistemic communities 'create reality, but not as they wish' (Adler and Haas 1992: 381). Haas (1992) argues that the ideas of an epistemic community have an impact on policy when experts reach positions of bureaucratic power, for example via the institutionalization of advisory committees that must be consulted before taking a decision. In assessing the epistemic community approach with the EU in mind, Richardson argues that the power of epistemic communities 'is constrained by the need for policy-makers – at the EU and national levels – to involve other forms of actors, particularly conventional interest groups' (Richardson 1996: 16). More generally, a strong case can be made for considering the members of a given epistemic community an actor (not the sole actor, and often not even the most powerful actor) in complex coalitions competing in functional policy areas. Of course, it all depends on the empirical case under examination. But, for example, it may well be that in a certain policy area there are two competing coalitions and one coalition is assisted by an underlying epistemic community (Radaelli 1997). The theoretical rationale for considering epistemic communities in their interplay with other actors is that knowledge and interests are in a symbiotic relation.

The presence of coalitions competing in functional areas and the role of uncertainty (and hence knowledge) suggest that the EU policy process can also be analysed by using the advocacy coalition framework developed by Sabatier (1998). This framework seeks to acknowledge up-front the symbiotic relation between knowledge and interests and aims at providing a model for empirical analysis. In Sabatier's own words:

> I have concluded that the most useful means of aggregating actors in order to understand policy change over fairly long periods of time is by advocacy coalitions. These are people from a variety of positions (elected and agency officials, interest group leaders, researchers, etc.) who share a particular belief system – that is, a set of basic values, causal assumptions, and problem perceptions – and who show a nontrivial degree of co-ordinated activity over time.
>
> (Sabatier 1993: 25)

If in the epistemic community approach the core concept is knowledge, the advocacy coalition approach focuses upon belief systems, which include knowledge, perceptions but also basic values.[16] Beliefs can be seen as the 'glue' which holds together a coalition (Sabatier 1993). Adversarial coalitions compete for the control of policy sub-systems. The result of the competition between coalitions, however, is not decided by power alone. Learning within (and, more rarely, across) coalitions and persuasion are at least as important as power. As Richardson notes, at least one of the hypotheses of this approach is relevant to the EU. Sabatier (1993; 1998) argues that policy-oriented learning across belief systems is more likely when there exists a forum which is prestigious enough to force professionals from different coalitions to participate and which is dominated by professional norms. Richardson observes that 'there is some evidence that Commission officials are moving towards institutionalised structures which do just this i.e. bring together groups of actors (be they epistemic communities, advocacy coalitions, or different policy communities) in a forum' (Richardson 1996: 18).

The Commission is then active in 'forum' politics (Coen 1997) and acts as a bourse of ideas and interests (Mazey and Richardson

1995). Instead of being a mere arena where member states play, the EU policy process is often a forum for discussions and negotiations. The Commission, by providing fora and managing learning processes, can reach a pivotal position in technocratic policy making. Summarizing, the analysis of the EU policy process in terms of actor-based models shows that knowledge and expertise matter in various ways. However, resources such as knowledge and tactics such as forum politics do not necessarily provide legitimacy to the initiatives of the Commission. Thus it is to the question of legitimacy that we now turn.

Technocratic legitimacy: three mechanisms of policy diffusion

'By almost any measure, the Commission fails the test of democratic legitimacy' (Featherstone 1994: 162). Yet the Commission – that is, the most technocratic body of the EU – has been able to play a very active role. One has therefore to explain how this expansion of tasks and competencies has occurred. As noted in Chapter Two, one of the main thrusts of technocracy (both as ideology and as a political project) is to secure legitimacy. The proposals of the Commission do not become European law unless the other institutions of the EU, most notably the Council of Ministers and the European Parliament agree to do so. Democratic legitimacy is a broad, multi-level concept (Weatherford 1992). It can be examined at the macro level[17] or by considering citizens' perceptions at the micro level.[18] In any case, it includes the fundamental consensus of the citizens (Beetham and Lord 1998; Schmitter 1998). But limited, 'technocratic' legitimacy for EU action is confined to the success of the Commission's proposals *vis-à-vis* the other institutions. I will use the term 'technocratic' legitimacy to designate actions which are considered legitimate within the formal perimeter of the EU policy process, thus excluding broader issues such as the consensus of citizens. How is technocratic legitimacy produced in the EU policy process? The previous analysis of the EU as a regulatory political system has shed light on the mechanisms of demand and supply (of regulation) that are instrumental in providing this type of legitimacy. The conceptual framework of policy transfer suggested by comparative politics and three mechanisms of institutional isomorphism (the tendency to become alike) provide supplementary insights on technocratic legitimacy. This section will introduce these three mechanisms.

Let us begin with policy diffusion (or policy transfer).[19] There is no need to illustrate the details of policy transfer. All the same, it is important to observe that it is a conceptual framework broad enough as to account for voluntary and coercive transfer, positive and negative lessons (that is, lessons about how not to proceed), transfer of wholesale policies and more limited transfer of instruments. For our purposes, the essential question is how policy transfer occurs in the EU.[20] The single most striking element of differentiation between policy transfer at the level of democratic states and supranational policy transfer in the EU concerns legitimacy. When a country decides to 'copy' one policy programme from another political system, it is legitimized in doing so by democratic rules and procedures, most notably elections. By contrast, EU institutions do not possess a similar degree of legitimacy.[21] Thus the following question arises: how does the EU – most notably, the Commission, which is the main policy initiator in the EU – secure legitimacy and diffuse policy? The literature on the tendency to become alike (also known as institutional isomorphism, Powell and DiMaggio 1991) draws our attention to three mechanisms: coercion, mimetism, and normative pressures.

Homogeneity in a competitive market is often the result of the search for efficiency. In political systems, however, 'organisations compete not just for resources and customers, but for political power and institutional legitimacy' (DiMaggio and Powell 1991: 66; see also Aldrich 1979). Copying organizational structures is not a process driven by efficiency considerations, but a way of securing legitimacy in institutional life. The adopted models may not enhance efficiency, but secure legitimacy. DiMaggio and Powell present three sources of homogenization: coercive, mimetic, and normative. Coercion is the response to such pressures as a government mandate or dependence on key organizations. For example, an organization will tend to become similar to those organizations on which it is dependent.

However, forces other than power and dependence can encourage imitation. This is the case of mimetism, which is triggered by uncertainty: 'when goals are ambiguous, or when the environment creates symbolic uncertainty, organisations may model themselves on other organisations' (DiMaggio and Powell 1991: 69).[22] Mimetism stems from the need to cope with uncertainty by imitating organizations which are perceived to be more legitimate or more successful. In this case again, imitation of models may not assure efficiency, but is nonetheless extremely effective in generating legitimacy.

In a paper on institutional design and democratic transitions, Offe has extended the idea of mimetism from organizations to institutions. Perceptively, he observes that 'institutional designs are typically copies, and are frequently advocated as such' (Offe 1992: 21). There is in fact a political advantage in claiming that one is copying rather than creating:

> The designer, if seen as such, will unavoidably come under the suspicion of trying to impose his particular interest or normative point of view upon the broader community, and that suspicion alone, unjustified though it may be in some cases, may invalidate the recognition and respect of the new institution.   (Offe 1992: 24)

Thus one should expect mimetism both under conditions of genuine uncertainty and as a political strategy. In both cases, the goal is to achieve legitimacy. Finally, normative pressures induced by professionalization represent the third ideal-type of isomorphic processes. Professionals, their associations and the mechanisms of formal education, socialization and recruitment, produce a common cognitive base which makes organizational structures similar one to another.

Turning to the EU, it can be observed that the first mechanism, coercion, is not likely to prevail, as there is no centralization of the policy process around a key organization. The pivotal role of the Commission is more a consequence of its role as an active bourse of interests and ideas than the result of member states' dependence on resources controlled by Brussels (Mazey and Richardson 1995). However, it should be noted that each member state is dependent on key resources produced by other member states: for example, the design of Economic and Monetary Union has diffused the German model for a variety of reasons, including the structural power of the Deutschmark as anchor currency (see Chapter Four).

Given the level of uncertainty that pervades EU policy making (Peters 1994; Richardson 1996), it can be argued that policy transfer in the EU should follow the path of mimetism in many circumstances. Finally, a variant of normative isomorphism can occur in those EU policy-making processes dominated by cognitive resources, expertise and even technocratic aspects of political life. An example is provided by the Delors Committee (examined in Chapter Four) which was instrumental in transmitting the beliefs of central bankers into the EU project for a single currency. Arguably, the political action of epistemic communities in the EU, albeit not equivalent to it, chimes with the consequences of normative isomorphism described by organizational theorists. In conclusion, one should expect to see the three mechanisms of technocratic legitimacy at work in the EU policy process, perhaps with more emphasis on mimetism than on coercion. Normative pressures become important when epistemic communities impact on EU public policy. The three case studies presented in the remainder of the book will generate empirical material for further elaboration on the issue of policy diffusion and technocratic legitimacy.

Conclusions

In this chapter, I have presented a synthetic overview of the politics of EU regulation, introduced actor-based models of the EU policy process, and presented three mechanisms of policy diffusion. There is a striking similarity between the original model of European integration and the technocratic bias of regulatory politics. Actor-based models, in addition, shed light on how experts, bureaucrats, and pressure groups interact. However, I do not think that one should conflate these elements into the concept of technocracy as outlined in Chapter Two. Of course, there are technocratic features both in the original model and in the present situation of EU public policy. However, it is not advisable to stretch the concept of technocracy so far as to cover epistemic communities, regulatory policy, and bureaucratic politics. For this reason I shall first assess the usefulness of technocracy by sticking to its original interpretation and then situate the more recent conceptualizations of the EU policy process by contrasting them with technocracy.

Let us begin with the concept of technocracy. As a catch-all concept, technocracy is a broad term which fits in rather well with many aspects of the EU. But upon closer investigation, the literature on technocracy does not appear very useful, especially when it points to the existence of a predictable economic environment guaranteed by the state (see Chapter Two). In brief, technocracy means big state, big planning, rationalization of the policy process

along predictable lines, and stabilization of the economy. However, the EU can be everything but big government (the EU
budget fluctuates under 1.5% of total EU GDP). In addition,
the EU policy process is considered very unstable (Peters 1994;
Richardson 1996).

Another critical point is that concepts such as technostructure
(Galbraith 1967), technocorporatism (Fischer 1990), the military-
industrial complex (Rosen 1973) or the technocomplex (Williams
1971) do not cover the same actors who are pivotal in the EU. Put
differently, the sociological scope of the previous concepts does
not apply to the EU easily. Policy making in the EU is fragmented,
'pillarized' and sectorialized: there is not such a thing as a uniform
bloc of power ruling the EU policy process (Peterson 1995b).

Turning to the arenas of power, EU politics is comprised of a
number of arenas. Studies of agenda setting in the EU have shed
light on several entry points for political demands. The Commission, the European Parliament, the European Court of Justice, but
also national political institutions are major arenas of EU politics.
So much so that actors engage in 'venue-shopping' (Richardson
1996; Sabatier 1998) and shift to the arena where they can best
employ their resources. The question then arises how can a technocratic class control all of these arenas? The plurality of arenas is a
very serious problem for technocratic theory.[23]

As far as ideology is concerned, technocracy can proliferate
under conditions of distrust of politicians. For technocracy to suc-
ceed, political decision making must be perceived as slow, corrupt,
and ultimately irrational. But the current ideological challenge in
the EU is all about people distrusting the 'bureaucrats of Brussels',
precisely because they are *not* political enough! If there is a political demand coming from public opinion, it is for more politics in
the EU policy process, not less.

In conclusion, technocratic theory is more a point of arrival
than a point of departure. Its major advantage is to adumbrate
certain areas of policy making where experts stabilize the policy-
making process by providing assumptions, rules, and models. However, as illustrated by Figure 3.2,[24] technocracy refers to policy
domains with both uncertainty and low political salience. If an
issue becomes politicized and yet remains uncertain, instead of the
smooth policy-making process described by technocratic theory,
one should expect a different political role of experts. This is where
the concept of epistemic community is useful. In fact, epistemic

47

Uncertainty

		Low	High
Salience	Low	Bureaucratic politics	Technocratic politics
	High	Political decision making	Epistemic communities

Figure 3.2 *Uncertainty and salience in the policy process*

communities impact on public policy under conditions of radical uncertainty *and* (a) conflict among actors who struggle to find out what their interest is on a given issue; and (b) a clear political role assigned to experts in the policy process. This is why Figure 3.2 assigns epistemic communities to the cell of high political salience and uncertainty. A result of the empirical literature, indeed, is that epistemic communities have played a key role in international environmental policy, a typical issue dominated by high political temperature amidst genuine uncertainty. The previous analysis, however, suggested that epistemic communities should not be examined in isolation, but preferably in the context of wider advocacy coalitions.

What happens when uncertainty is not a relevant aspect of the policy process? Under these conditions, it can be hypothesized that the competition for power, instead of learning, becomes of paramount importance. Organizations pursue reflexive goals and, if political salience is low (and accordingly the issue is neglected by high-level politicians), bureaucratic politics should prevail, as shown in Figure 3.2. Expertise remains significant, but, more importantly still, bureaucracies will fight for expanding their competencies in a classic turf battle. It can be hypothesized, for example, that different Directorates of the Commission will compete for setting the agenda in their favourite terms, or that the European Parliament will argue against the Council not in terms of the merit of a specific proposal, but for reasserting its agenda setting powers. In short, the politics of bureaucratic competition instead of the politics of learning.

Finally, the arena of political decision making should not be neglected. This chapter deals with the technocratic aspects of the EU policy process, but there are issues of high-politics and history-making decisions that fit in nicely with our conventional knowledge of politics (Peterson 1995b). Traditional politics is still enormously important in the EU. Think of intergovernmental bargains, national party leaders and prime ministers at the EU table, and ideological conflicts (for example, the social market economy paradigm versus classic liberal economic policy) in EU labour policy and social policy.

Political decision making, as indicated by Figure 3.2, requires a reduction of uncertainty. In turn, uncertainty can be reduced either objectively or subjectively. An objective reduction of uncertainty takes place when the frontier of knowledge advances. An example of this objective reduction of uncertainty is when conclusive studies show that certain policies (that is, urban policies or pension policies) are no longer compatible with demographic trends. Politics, however, is also an exercise in interpretation of an ambiguous, often elusive reality. Policy makers can stabilize the assumptions needed for political action by using paradigms, narratives and conceptual frameworks which simplify a complex reality and make social problems amenable to public policy. As will be shown in Chapter Five, the adoption of tax competition as the yardstick for EU tax policy has reduced uncertainty in a subjective way. Objective uncertainty in tax policy remains high, but the threat of tax competition destroying the single market, the welfare state and employment provides sufficient reasons to proceed. Among tax policy makers, there is no subjective uncertainty about the need to take action against tax competition (see Chapter Five).

Having clarified the main concepts for the analysis of the EU policy making, one has to investigate empirically issues such as technocracy, epistemic communities and the question of low versus high political salience. The remainder of the book is dedicated to these issues in the context of three case studies. The single currency will be examined first, before proceeding to the analysis of tax policy and media ownership policy.

Notes

1 Jean Monnet was the first president of the High Authority (1951–55), the body which in many respects can be considered the predecessor of the Commission. On his role and legacy see Featherstone (1994) and Monnet's memoirs (Monnet 1978).

2 In 1957 the founding treaties of the European Community (called the European Union since 1992), separately establishing the European Economic Community (EEC) and the European Atomic Energy Community (Euratom), were signed in Rome (and are therefore referred to as the 'Treaty of Rome'). The Treaty of Rome has since been revised three times: in 1987 (the Single Act), in 1992 (the Treaty on European Union at Maastricht) and in 1997 (the Treaty of Amsterdam).

3 Fulvio Attinà reminded me that the early stage was also marked by an intense intellectual activity in favour of the democratization of the integration process. Technocracy and democratization were thus simultaneously present in the debate. But there was only one incarnation of the many designs for the ECSC and the European Economic Community, and this was a technocratic one.

4 Being mainly concerned with coal and steel policy, the High Authority had a completely different policy domain than the Commission we know nowadays.

5 Page however draws attention to the fact that the High Authority was modelled along the lines of the League of Nations Secretariat and the Secretariat of the United Nations (Page 1997: 6).

6 Typically, regulatory policy is a response to market failures. Its main rationale is to re-establish efficiency when market failures operate (Breyer 1982; Coase 1937; Pigou 1932).

7 For a more theoretical treatment of the problem of delegation see Pollack (1997). From different perspectives, Shapiro (1997) and Egan (1998) show that the clash of interests and political controversies are not dissolved by delegation. Thus delegation represents a possible solution to the credibility dilemma, but not the end of political struggle.

8 This emphasis is important. For it is well known that when it comes to implementing EU policies, governments and public administrations often find themselves facing costs. What I am referring to here is the perception of costs in the decisional stage.

9 To complete the demand picture, it should be added that in some circumstances countries accept EU public policy as a way to get out of politically difficult national situations. These are the circumstances where European measures are a useful scapegoat, a way of avoiding

direct political responsibilities in difficult areas like cutting back industries with excess capacity or structural readjustment of public finance (Dyson and Featherstone 1996a). Summarizing, the external obligation adequately protects governments from the accusation of seeking to penalize their own citizens and firms.

10 On the policy entrepreneurship of the Commission see Cram (1993), George (1995), and the mechanisms of 'policy-making by subterfuge' described by Heritier (1997).

11 I am grateful to Giuliano Amato for having pointed this out to me in conversation.

12 See however the profound change in the politics of regulation over the last twenty years, as illustrated by regulatory reforms in all OECD countries (OECD 1997).

13 See Allison (1971), Downs (1967) and Peters (1992). For a comprehensive typology of bureaucratic activity see Page (1997: Chapter 7).

14 An organization has purposive goals when it seeks to achieve policy objectives, reflexive goals when it is concerned with the expansion of its own power, budget, prestige or reputation.

15 For more elaboration on this, see Radaelli (1995; 1997 Chapters 2 and 9)

16 Agreement over policy core beliefs is – according to Sabatier (1998: 105) – the 'glue holding a coalition together'. *Policy core* beliefs are 'fundamental policy positions concerning the basic strategies for achieving core values' (Sabatier 1998: 112). They include normative and empirical precepts. Policy core beliefs with an empirical component define, for example, the overall seriousness of a policy problem, the causes of the problem, and the proper distribution of authority among levels of government (Sabatier 1998: 112). By contrast, *secondary* beliefs concern instrumental decisions necessary to implement the policy core, and *deep core* beliefs are at the level of ontological axioms and fundamental norms. According to Sabatier, policy learning across belief systems is limited to secondary beliefs. The policy core can change as well, but not as an effect of learning. Rather, a perturbation in non-cognitive factors external to the policy area (for example, a shock in the policy environment which alters the balance of resources between adversarial coalitions) is the trigger of change in policy core beliefs. As major policy change requires modification of the policy core, Sabatier concludes that cognitive factors are not likely to produce dramatic policy shift.

17 According to Weatherford (1992), the macro perspective on legitimacy stands on four attributes: accountability, efficiency, procedural fairness, and distributive fairness.

18 That is, by dint of surveys measuring attributes such as the perception of political and personal efficacy, personal trust, political interest, and citizen duties. See Weatherford (1992) for an integrated model covering both the macro and the micro perspective.

19 Diffusion is 'the process by which an innovation spreads . . . It consists of the communication of a new idea in a social system over time' (Gray 1973: 1175). Earlier studies focused on diffusion (Gray 1973; Walker 1969). The recent discussion, instead, tends to opt for the terminology of transfer and lesson-drawing. See Dolowitz and Marsh (1996) and their discussion of similarities and differences between policy transfer and lesson-drawing as introduced by Rose (1991; 1993). Typically, the literature on the EU associates policy transfer with the dissemination of technology, but in this book the concept of EU policy transfer is broader. In fact, it refers to the transfer of policy competencies from member states to European institutions. As such, policy transfer, in this study, is all about the creation and diffusion of EU public policy, and about the legitimacy of the Commission's initiatives within the EU policy process.

20 For a broader discussion of policy transfer in the EU see my paper on the Jean Monnet Chair site at the University of Catania: http://www.fscpo.unict.it/vademec/jmwp10.htm.

21 For different approaches to the concept of political legitimacy see Dogan (1992), Barker (1990) and Beetham (1991). On legitimacy in the EU the reader can compare Banchoff and Smith (1998), Drake (1997), Matlary (1997), Obradovic (1996), Weiler (1992), and the comprehensive treatment offered by Beetham and Lord (1998).

22 In a recent critique of DiMaggio and Powell, Czarniawska (1997: 186 emphasis in original) argues that mimetic processes should be 'interpreted in terms of *fashion* (a social phenomenon) rather than of imitation·(a cognitive process)'.

23 Page (1997: 3–4) observes that 'in the decision-making structure of the European Union it is very difficult to talk of any one body, group, or individual holding power, if the term power refers to a long-term capacity to determine what laws the EU should pass or on what EU money should be spent'.

24 The typology proposed in Figure 3.2 is only an initial step in order to present my arguments as clearly as possible. It should be considered as a device for stressing the need to differentiate among technocracy, bureaucratic politics, epistemic communities and political processes in the EU.

CHAPTER FOUR

The single currency:
who won at Maastricht?

Introduction

On 7 February 1992 the foreign and finance ministers of the European Community convened at Maastricht to sign the Treaty on the European Union, thus assigning constitutional status to a series of precepts for the single currency. The design of monetary union enshrined in the monetary provision of the Treaty on the European Union[1] includes the following key points:

- a three-stage process towards the single currency, with the qualification that only countries respecting criteria of nominal convergence[2] (inflation, currency stability, public deficit and public debt) would make it into the final stage;
- the choice of price stability as the overriding policy objective of the Euro;
- the surrender of national sovereignty in monetary policy to a fully independent European Central Bank;
- tight rules prohibiting the European Central Bank from bailing out countries with fiscal imbalances.[3]

The Economic and Monetary Union (EMU) represents one of the most important progresses in European integration, a quantum leap with profound implications for the member countries, the citizens of the EU, and the global financial scene. The question of 'who won at Maastricht' is therefore an important component of our understanding of the changing power relations in Europe. It is however impossible to provide a straightforward answer to this question and say for example, as tabloid wisdom often has it, that Germany or the Franco-German axis imposed their preferences during the intergovernmental negotiations. As will be shown in this chapter, the EMU policy process is an extremely complex one: bargaining at Maastricht was nothing but one of the decisive factors at work. Other important aspects of the EMU policy process include the web of structural relations within which political action is embedded,[4] the linkages between EMU and domestic politics,[5] and the agency of supranational institutions, notably the European Commission and its then entrepreneurial President, Jacques Delors (Dyson and Featherstone 1997).

However, the main goal in this chapter is not to present yet another model of the 'politics of Maastricht'.[6] Rather, the aim is to take seriously the hypothesis of technocracy as the major drive in the European policy process and to assess whether it is plausible and makes sense in the case of EMU. A limitation of the analytic scope is needed, however. Unforeseen contingencies and intense, even incendiary, political (as opposed to technocratic) debates took place post-Maastricht, starting with the Danish referendum rejecting the Treaty on the European Union in 1992 and the notorious black Wednesday on 16 September 1992. Those events plagued (albeit they did not derail it) what Sandholtz has dubbed Europe's rough road to monetary union (Sandholtz 1996). Therefore, the hypothesis of a technocratic policy process governing EMU from the beginning to the historic decision to admit eleven countries to the single currency in May 1998 would be simply untenable. With hindsight, it is all too clear that political forces, and not technocratic power, have shaped the road to the single currency.

But the technocratic hypothesis seems more promising for describing the creation of EMU, that is, the policy process that led to the monetary provisions included in the Treaty on the European Union signed at Maastricht. All in all, EMU scholars have been amazed by the extraordinary technicalities of this policy, the degree of technical consensus surrounding key political decisions such as Treaty making, and the pivotal position of economists and central bankers. Verdun, for example, qualifies as puzzling the fact that 'consensus on the creation of EMU in the Community could have been reached so easily' and adds that 'the general public started to show considerable interest in the EMU project only after the Treaty had been signed' (Verdun 1997: 1–2). Dyson goes even further. In his critique of the limitations of the Treaty on the European Union, he argues that the élite-level policy debate became trapped in a one-dimensional view rooted in the belief that it was possible, desirable and sufficient to base the European Monetary System and the Economic and Monetary Union on technical ideas of 'sound money' and to encapsulate those ideas in a treaty.   (Dyson 1994: 6)

However, how can the technocratic hypothesis be assessed empirically? The chapter proceeds in four steps. First, a cursory overview of the events is presented. Second, the technocratic hypothesis will be articulated in the form of the power of economic ideas and policy paradigms. Third, attention will be switched from ideas to actors, and the question will be raised whether actors with policy-relevant knowledge (such as economists and central bankers) were instrumental in shaping the Treaty on the European Union. In this context, the case for an epistemic community steering the EMU policy process will be introduced and critically discussed. Finally, I will present my own conclusion: although economic models and communities of experts were extremely important in addressing issues of technical feasibility and in shaping options at key junctures, the creation of EMU cannot be interpreted as a victory of technocracy or epistemic communities. As shown in Chapter Three, technocracy and epistemic communities do not exclude any notion of politics.[7] Quite the opposite, they represent two forms in which knowledge can become the terrain of politics. Therefore I will examine the politics of expertise in the case of EMU and contrast it with political decision-making as defined in Chapter 3.

To sum up then, the structure of the chapter can be articulated in the following questions:

- *EMU and technocratic ideas.* Does the Treaty on the European Union (more precisely, the parts concerning EMU) encapsulate a paradigm of monetary policy? Can it be considered the political victory of an economic school? Is EMU the optimal solution, in terms of economic theory, to the problems of currency fluctuations and economic instability of the EU?
- *EMU and technocratic actors.* Is the Treaty consistent with the preferences of actors possessing knowledge as their fundamental resource? If so, who are these actors?
- *Alternatives to technocratic hypotheses.* Did political decision making prevail over economic paradigms and communities of experts, and if so how?

The road to Maastricht

The idea of a monetary union in Europe was not created at Maastricht. Indeed, it is an idea dating back to the late 1960s, when Pierre Werner, Prime Minister and Finance Minister of Luxembourg, launched the idea of a single currency. At that time, the European Economic Community was completing the removal of internal tariffs and was putting the finishing touches to the new complicated price mechanisms of the Common Agricultural Policy.[8] Suppressing exchange rate volatility – argued the Vice President of the Commission Raymond Barre, who endorsed Werner's key proposal, although dissenting on other points[9] – was a necessary step towards a stronger Community, both internally[10] and in relation to non-European currencies. The Community, in fact, was proceeding swiftly towards greater trade interdependence and the monetary problems of autumn–winter 1968 illustrated how sensitive individual countries had become to international monetary turbulence.

In December 1969 the then six leaders of the European Community met in the city of The Hague. In a climate of cooperation, to be recollected later as 'the spirit of The Hague' (Dyson 1994: 76–9; Rosenthal 1975: Chapter 7), the leaders agreed that 'a plan in stages should be worked out during 1970 with a view to the creation of an economic and monetary union'.[11] Accordingly, the summit of The Hague set up a working group on EMU, chaired by Werner, entrusted with the submission of a report on EMU. The Council accepted the Report of the Werner committee, dubbed the Werner Report, in 1971.

A line of disagreement became evident soon within the Werner committee and more generally among European countries. This cleavage – commonly known as *economists versus monetarists*[12] – is important because it structured the early politics of EMU and remained almost intact up until the negotiations at Maastricht. What does it consist of? Simply put, economists believe that a substantial degree of economic convergence and coordination should precede the irrevocable fixity of parities. In a word, economic coordination comes first. Monetarists (or institutionalists), by contrast, argue that the EMU strategy should commence with the establishment of common monetary institutions (for example a central bank) prior to effective coordination. The arrow of causation goes from institutions to economic coordination. Institutions – monetarists argue

– shape market behaviour and in turn trigger convergence. A corollary is that for economists a firm date for the single currency does not make sense: the elimination of currency fluctuations should take place only when economies converge, and it is impossible to speculate on the date of convergence in advance. For monetarists, an EMU fixed date is instead part and parcel of the institution-driven path to convergence.

Let us examine how the two adversarial beliefs reverberated in the discussion preceding the Werner Report. As illustrated by Tsoukalis (1977: 90–1), 'already at The Hague summit, it had become apparent that the desirability of an EMU as the final objective, shared by both President Pompidou and Chancellor Brandt, did not stop the two leaders from having different priorities for the initial stage'. While the German Chancellor insisted on the coordination of economic policies as a prerequisite for any progress towards EMU,[13] the French President seemed to be more interested in immediate measures in the monetary field and in setting up the foundations for the creation of a regional monetary bloc. In 1970, Germany and the Netherlands were the champions among the economists, with a certain support from Italy.[14] Instead, France, Belgium and Luxembourg were firmly in the camp of the monetarists. Twenty years later, in a Community of twelve members, the same cleavage resurfaced, to show the fundamental persistence of divergent views of EMU. Of the original six members, only Italy had somewhat changed position, by sitting on the monetarists' side of the table at Maastricht.

Faced with this cleavage, the Werner Report struck a compromise, albeit one ultimately tilted towards the preferences of the 'economists'. The Report introduced the principle of a symmetric EMU, also known as the principle of parallelism, to denote parallel progress in the economic and monetary dimensions. It envisaged the creation of an economic institution – the centre of decision for economic policy – as well as a monetary institution – the community system for central banks. The idea of Economic *and* Monetary Union developed a deeper meaning, after having being debated by experts who were deeply divided about the appropriate road to follow. Although, 'in a diplomatic sense, the principle of parallelism stood as a symbol of the compromise between monetarists and economists', 'the substantive content of the report betrayed the degree of German policy leadership' (Dyson 1994: 81). In fact, the Report recommended specific steps in the achievement of substantive economic policy convergence before realizing EMU. In addition, the Werner Report considered EMU a leaven for the development of the political union, a typical goal of the German government.

An essential component of the compromise was the so-called guillotine clause. The clause provided a first stage of parallel progress in economic and monetary union, to last for four years. If at the end of this stage agreement on the final shape of EMU would not emerge, then the mechanisms of monetary policy coordination would cease to apply. As the Dutch secretary of state for foreign affairs put it: 'we are like the couple who have an engagement party. If over the next five years we don't get married, we return the gifts' (quoted by Rosenthal 1975: 111). For Germany, this deal secured that EMU could have been stopped, had economic policy coordination failed to perform well.

As known, the three-stage approach to EMU envisaged by the Werner Report crashed against the currency instability of the early 1970s. In a context of dramatic turbulence, in 1971 Nixon declared the inconvertibility of dollars and gold. Between 1971 and 1973 the whole worldwide exchange rate regime collapsed. But the vicissitudes of The Hague and the Werner Report are important for three reasons. First, they forged the imprint of the EMU policy process, with the cleavage between institutionalists and economists emerging as the main polarization. Second, the Report originated the idea of a gradual approach to EMU, based upon the completion of three different stages. Third, the EMU policy process crystallized around a community of monetary experts and officials. They were not selected only because of their technical expertise. Indeed, they were selected in such a way as to make sure that member states were all represented by an outstanding expert. This element of member state representation was not predominant, however. More important was the fact that these experts felt part of the same professional world. As illustrated by the pioneering study conducted by Glenda Rosenthal (1975) on 'the men behind the decisions', EMU, as fleshed out in the early 1970s, was more the product of a 'network élite' – as she put it – than the result of intergovernmental bargaining or group and parliamentary pressure.[15] She described this network as:

> a community of experts and technocrats, most of whom knew each other well, many of whom had been trained at the same schools,

worked at very similar jobs (either in their national capitals or in EEC headquarters in Brussels), attended the same meetings all over the world – in short, a small, exclusive community of experts within a larger community, the European Economic Community.

(Rosenthal 1975: 124)

Was EMU predestined to evolve in the shadow of technocracy?

When the monetary storms of 1971–73 shattered the grandiose hopes for EMU, the European countries decided to erect a bulwark against the destabilization of currencies and the two-digit inflation. Enormously less ambitious than the EMU, the so-called snake (this was the name of the bulwark) was a mechanism designed to curb fluctuations against each other's currency within a grid of 2.25 per cent. The problem with the snake was that it lacked mechanisms of coordinated intervention (such as support and negotiations of new realignments) when a currency was reaching the lower level of the grid. Hence when currencies touched the bottom of the grid they simply dropped out of the snake. It happened to the Irish punt and the British pound in 1972, to the lira in 1973 and to the French franc twice, in 1974 and 1976. A two-tier monetary system had therefore evolved (Dyson 1994: 93).

Unsurprisingly, the Werner plan for EMU was shelved and political efforts were focused on how to improve the snake. A solution was found in 1979 with the European Monetary System (EMS)[16] and, within the EMS, the Exchange Rate Mechanism.[17] At the beginning, the effectiveness of the EMS appeared in doubt (with seven realignments in the first four years!) but later the EMS performed well. Inflation rates converged in Europe and 'the widespread perception was that the EMS could provide external stability to countries seeking price stability' (Sandholtz 1993: 28).[18]

Given this satisfactory performance, the question arises why did European countries decide to move beyond the EMS? The initiative came from different sides. To begin with, some countries perceived the EMS as asymmetric in that the burden of adjustment fell disproportionately upon the weak currencies. The bone of contention was that under the EMS regime the stronger countries were systematically undervalued. In turn, this produced large surpluses in the international trade transactions for countries such as Germany, whose currency (and behind it the Bundesbank) had become the powerful anchor of the EMS. During the first decade of the EMS, Germany earned a cumulative surplus of more than

$200 billion in its trade with other European Community countries (Cameron 1995: 44). Britain, France and Italy experienced large cumulative deficits.[19]

French minister Edouard Balladur advanced his critique to the EMS in 1988[20] and called upon the Community members to improve the mechanisms of monetary cooperation.[21] He went so far as to propose a discussion on the single currency, and, not surprisingly, this idea found a warm reception among the partners with weak currencies. The Italian Minister Giuliano Amato hastened to circulate a paper critical of the asymmetric features of the EMS.[22] Other countries – such as Greece, Ireland, Portugal and Spain – supported the initial idea of moving beyond the EMS. Their intention was to soften the EMS, by maintaining a credible commitment to low inflation and sound money, 'but without having to suffer the full consequences of the Bundesbank's uncompromising policy stance' (Garrett 1993: 113).

The French initiative was echoed, somewhat surprisingly, by the German Foreign Minister, Hans Dietrich Genscher, who presented a paper on 'a European currency area and a European Central Bank' (26 February 1988). Genscher, a passionate European federalist, stressed the advantages of a single currency and a European Central Bank in terms of the completion of the single market, less dependence on the dollar, and price stability in Europe. Genscher's position was not accepted without hesitation within the German government. Finance Minister Gerhard Stoltenberg, for example, was less keen on heading towards a single currency than Genscher. However, Genscher's position was inherently stronger than Stoltenberg's, for three reasons.

To begin with, during the first six months of 1988 Germany held the European Presidency. This implies that the Foreign Minister was chairing European Council meetings. Second, the German government (Stoltenberg included) was aware of the importance of capital movement liberalization. The Council was agreeing upon a proposal for a liberalizing directive in 1988. A consequence of capital movement liberalization was that the EMS could not have worked as well as in the past. The logic of pegged yet adjustable exchange rates – in other words, periods of currency stability followed by episodic realignments – was tenable only in the presence of capital controls. The latter protected central bank reserves from speculative attacks originated by expectations of realignments. As shown below, this argument was considered a cogent reason for the revision of the EMS. Third, Genscher's initiative was rooted in the Franco-German collaboration based on the goals of pro-gressive rapprochement and the Franco-German axis as the core of European integration. In 1987–88 there emerged a 'high-level political understanding' between Kohl and Mitterrand, on the one hand, and Genscher and his French counterpart Dumas, that 'con-tinued German monetary policy autonomy and consequent French dependency were, in the long term, incompatible with these two twin objectives' (Dyson and Featherstone 1996b: 332–3).

Apart from the Franco-German protagonists (Mitterrand and Balladur, Genscher and Kohl), the European Commission, headed by Jacques Delors, was pushing for the single currency. Delors would have liked to link EMU to his first successful project, the Single European Act, but in 1986 he could muster consensus only on a mention to EMU in the preamble to the Single European Act. Two years later, the situation looked more promising for the Com-mission's long standing goal to advance monetary cooperation up until the creation of a single currency. The so-called Padoa-Schioppa Report[23] was requested by the Commission in 1986. It provided ammunition for the Commission in that it made the case for the revision of institutional mechanisms of monetary policy coordina-tion following the liberalization of capital movement. The Padoa-Schioppa Report did not advocate for a fast move to EMU, but was influential – Dyson (1994: 118–19) explains – because of

> its insistence on a fundamental contradiction between the retention of independent monetary policies, on the one hand, and retention of stable exchange rates in the new framework of capital mobility, on the other. In the end, a key weapon of monetary authorities in the face of speculative attacks in the markets – exchange controls – was being removed. It was a message that enjoyed significant influ-ence in Council bargaining and gave a new cogency and sense of purpose to economic arguments for a relaunch of EMU.

This argument was summarized by Padoa-Schioppa as the 'incon-sistent quartet' argument (see Padoa-Schioppa 1988: 373–6). The Community – Padoa-Schioppa asserted – would not work with four properties simultaneously active: a single market for goods, capital liberalization, fixed exchange rates, and national monetary policy autonomy.

Genscher, in his capacity as chair of the Council of Ministers for the first half of 1988, prepared the agenda for the Hanover

European Council (June 1988), a turning point in the path to
EMU. In fact, at Hanover the European leaders discussed the idea
of a European Central Bank, with Mitterrand, Delors, Genscher
and Balladur amongst the keenest supporters of the proposal
(Thatcher, by contrast, abhorring it). Kohl took a middle position,
stating that in any case a possible European Central Bank would
have to be fully independent from political pressures, very much
on the line of the German Bundesbank. The Hanover summit final-
ized with no explicit reference to the European Central Bank. This
pleased the UK Prime Minister, but a more important decision had
already been made, that is, the decision to establish a committee
of experts – acting independently in their personal capacity – chaired
by Jacques Delors. The committee included two members from the
Commission (its chair and the Commissioner in charge of external
relations), three independent experts, and twelve members of the
Committee of Central Bank Governors. The Committee – it was
agreed at Hanover – would study, and make proposals for, 'concrete stages leading to the progressive realisation of EMU'.

Within the Delors Committee,[24] the old cleavage between
economists and monetarists resurfaced (Cameron 1995: 48) and
was bound to characterize the entire intergovernmental conference
on EMU (Dyson and Featherstone 1997: 21). The Bundesbank was
yet again the pivotal actor within the economist coalition (flanked
by the British, Dutch, and Luxembourg bankers within the Delors
Committee), whereas Delors and the bankers from countries such
as France and Italy led the monetarist coalition. The final report of '
the Delors Committee[25] – with a striking similarity to the former
Werner Report – recommended a three-stage process leading to
EMU. It also argued for economic convergence to be achieved
before switching to a single currency and common monetary institutions (such as a European Central Bank). Along this vein, the
Report did not set any end-date for the achievement of the single
currency. As such, the economists' view was to prevail. The Report
of the Delors Committee, Cameron observes (1995: 50), 'established the broad parameters of EMU as it eventually appeared in
the Treaty on European Union'. Therefore, in the following section we will examine the role of this Committee in more detail
and discuss the question whether this Committee operated like an
epistemic community. But now let us proceed with the narrative.

In the aftermath of the publication of the Delors Committee
Report, the European Prime Ministers and heads of state convened

in Madrid (June 1989) and Strasbourg (December 1989). The outcome of these summits was the decision to convene an intergovernmental conference on EMU, due to start in December 1990. This proposal was submitted formally by Mitterrand to the Strasbourg European Council and was approved by all countries with the lone exception of the UK. One important reason for Kohl's vote in favour of Mitterrand's proposal was his concern with German re-unification. Cameron (1995: 57), for example, refers to the tacit bargaining between Kohl's agreement on the EMU intergovernmental conference and the Strasbourg declaration supporting German re-unification. Therefore Kohl's political objectives distanced him from the position of the Bundesbank, which was extremely cautious in proceeding with a fast track to EMU.

The intergovernmental conference was prepared by the Monetary Committee, a body of the European Community composed of the deputy ministers of finance and the deputy governors of the central banks of the member states. During an informal meeting of finance ministers and central bankers at Ashford Castle, it was decided that the European Central Bank would be politically independent (following the suggestion of the Delors Report) and that devaluation would be excluded as a means of adjustment within EMU. This commitment to price stability and central bank independence reflected the preferences of the Bundesbank. Finally, the proposal to accompany EMU with additional regional aid was rejected at Ashford Castle. An implication of this decision was the shift of the poorer European countries towards a more cautious position on EMU.

The second half of 1990 was characterized by two crucial dynamics, one related to the Bundesbank and another concerning the positions of different member states. The President of the Bundesbank, Karl Otto Pöhl, raised four points, which were to mark the final outcome of EMU. First, he argued for the possibility of a two-speed EMU. Not all countries – he stated – would progress into the single currency, but only those with their economic fundamentals in order. Second, he insisted on central bank independence as *the* indispensable pre-condition for a successful EMU, fending off the attack of those who favoured a *gouvernement economique,* a formula which, in various guises, entailed the establishment of a political power to counterbalance the European Central Bank. Third, Pöhl used the daunting problems of Germany's monetary unification as a warning against a too fast transition to

EMU in the absence of considerable economic convergence. A corollary of this position was that there should be no transition timetable. Transition would take place if and only if European economies would converge towards low inflation and economic stability. And fourth, the Bundesbank issued its own proposals for the decisive second stage of EMU (the transitional stage before the introduction of fixed parities) and suggested that convergence criteria should be respected by countries willing to join the single currency. Incidentally, during the months of Pöhl's offensive, the Committee of Central Bank Governors was drafting the statute of the European Central Bank: the model of the Bundesbank represented the most powerful source of inspiration in this drafting exercise.

The second event was a bitter confrontation between two conceptions of EMU, that is, the 'go slow' versus the 'fast track' (Cameron 1995). The old cleavage between economists and monetarists reverberated underneath this confrontation. In fact, the advocates of the slow approach to EMU were insisting on the need to first qualify in terms of economic convergence (hence the relevance of quantitative criteria as suggested by the Bundesbank) and then proceed to the creation of common institutions for monetary policy and the single currency. On the fast trackers' side, Delors proposed an early transition to a short second stage of EMU. France, Italy and Belgium supported him, but ultimately his proposal was rejected. Delors spoke of the emergence of 'a sort of rejection front ... those who want an economic and monetary union so beautiful, so perfect, that it will never get started, it will never be born' (quoted by Cameron 1995: 66).

However, the emergence of a majority of cautious economists (as opposed to the fast tracker monetarists) was already a fact. Spain, and with this country the other poorer members of the Community, left the monetarist coalition. The decision to exclude further regional aid taken at Ashford left countries such as Spain with the options of being included in the second tier of the two-speed EMU, or being forced to enact harsh economic policy programmes in order to catch up with the virtuosity of the best European economies in terms of inflation and sound public finance. Both options were less than enthralling and consequently Spain took the lead of a massive defection of poorer countries from the monetarists' camp.

The intergovernmental conference on EMU opened in Rome in December 1990 and was concluded in Maastricht in December

1991. The conference was dedicated to the negotiation of the treaty.[26] As early as February 1991, three months after the beginning of the conference, Germany submitted a draft of a complete EMU treaty, prepared in close consultation with the Bundesbank (Cameron 1995). The draft embodied a series of principles which were due to be adopted at Maastricht, most crucially stringent economic criteria on inflation and public finance, the two-speed design of EMU, and the creation of an independent European Central Bank in stage three (not before, as the monetarists would have wished).[27]

These principles were echoed in the draft treaty submitted subsequently by the Dutch presidency of the European Community during the second half of 1991. The Bundesbank supported publicly the Dutch draft treaty, against the opposition of the Commission, Italy, Belgium and Greece. The final Dutch proposal was presented to the Committee of Central Bank Governors and eventually submitted for approval to the intergovernmental conference. An important concession to the Commission and the other fast trackers was the decision to let the third stage of EMU begin in any case no later than 1 January 1999.[28] For the rest, in December 1991 the twelve leaders of the Community agreed to an EMU design based on 'economic convergence first', independence of the European Central Bank, and 'no bail out' rules for countries in economic difficulties. As mentioned, the Treaty of the European Union was signed at Maastricht in February 1992.

The economic case for EMU and the role of economic policy paradigms

After this cursory view at how EMU materialized at Maastricht, we turn our attention to two different themes connected to the politics of expertise. The first revolves around the question as to whether there is an economic case for EMU. The second posits that the driving force behind EMU was an economic policy paradigm consistent with the preferences of the monetary 'mandarins', essentially central bankers, but also technocrats working in Finance Ministries and Commission's officials. The key question is who was empowered by EMU?

Let us begin with the first theme. The theme of an economic rationale for EMU has been articulated in various forms. Most importantly, perhaps, the gospel of the 'inconsistent quartet' mentioned above. Put differently, this is an argument about the functional necessity of EMU. If Europe wants to enjoy the benefits of the single market – inclusive of free capital movement – it has to surrender domestic monetary autonomy. The Delors Report (CSEMU 1989: 16) stressed the functional necessity of EMU by arguing that EMU would be 'in many respects a natural consequence of the commitment to create a market without frontiers'.[29] The emphasis, of course, is on the word 'natural'.

However, economic analysis (Eichengreen 1997; Giavazzi *et al.* 1988) has demonstrated that there is nothing 'natural' in the choice of complementing an integrated trade area with a single currency. For such an area could even thrive on the competition among different currencies. Indeed, currency competition could keep inflation low. In Eichengreen's words: 'no strictly economic obstacle prevents countries from removing trade barriers and restructuring along lines of comparative advantage while retaining national, potentially fluctuating, currencies' (Eichengreen 1997: 247). So much so – Eichengreen continues (1997: 323) – that the case for monetary unification must be advanced on *political* grounds rather than on considerations of economic efficiency. Indeed, it is doubtful that the elimination of exchange rate uncertainty is the 'natural' way to promote European trade and investment. Economic studies[30] show that exchange rate variability does not necessarily trigger perverse effects on trade and investment. Quite the opposite, if financial markets are efficient, the variability of exchange rates should be an incentive to investors to hold diversified portfolios of assets. And there is nothing wrong with portfolio diversification, especially if financial markets are flexible and open. Hence there would be no negative impact in terms of efficiency. Concluding on this point, a simplistic, spillover-type, argument positing a natural linkage between the single currency and EMU appears to be flawed.

Another proposition about the efficiency of EMU has been advanced throughout the years, namely that the introduction of the single currency would bring efficiency because of the elimination of currency conversion costs. With the introduction of the Euro, the costs of converting French francs into German Deutschmarks will be eliminated. However, these costs are on average 0.4 per cent of the EU gross domestic product.[31] Nobody could seriously argue that this economic gain outweighs the political cost implied in the loss of monetary policy autonomy!

A more consistent, yet ultimately unconvincing, economic rationale for EMU stems from the theory of optimum currency areas.[32] The theory lays down the conditions under which the establishment of a currency union is an optimal economic strategy. In particular, the literature pins down two important prerequisites for a successful optimum currency area: labour flexibility and the presence of intergovernmental fiscal flows, which compensate for shocks affecting a sub-area of the union.[33] Let us consider how these mechanisms work and assume first that a country can use the exchange rate as an instrument of economic policy. When a country faces an asymmetric shock, the most typical instrument of adjustment is via the exchange rate.[34] For example, a country suffering from a temporary lack of demand can respond by means of a devaluation, which will raise the level of exports. But if exchange rate variability is suppressed because of the establishment of a monetary union, workers are requested to move from the area of the monetary union wherein the asymmetric shock took place to another. Alternatively, a system of fiscal federalism can automatically redistribute income to areas of the monetary union badly hit by an economic shock.

How does the EU match the profile of an optimal area for a single currency? One of the key features of the Maastricht Treaty is the lack of fiscal federalism. The Werner Report contemplated a dual system of economic *and* monetary union, but the EMU which materialized at Maastricht is very much a monetary union bereft of mechanisms for fiscal adjustment. As for labour mobility, the best way to assess the EU is to compare it with existing monetary unions, such as the USA and Canada. On this point, accurate and systematic economic studies conclude that the EU does not score as well as the USA and Canada (Eichengreen 1997: Chapter 3). This means that if there is a monetary union approaching the ideal of an optimum currency area, it is not likely to be the EU.[35]

EMU does not necessarily represent an optimal choice in terms of economic theory. Thus an economic case for EMU cannot be made in these terms. However, this does not imply that economic policy paradigms did not matter throughout the path to EMU. Indeed, EMU clearly embodies an economic paradigm of central bank independence and overriding commitment to price stability. More precisely, this is the paradigm that Marcussen (1997) has dubbed as 'sound money, sound inflation, and sound finances'.[36] The statute of the European Central Bank resembles closely the one of the German Bundesbank. And during the negotiations, 'on the issue of central bank independence German negotiators did not have to seek out a leadership role' (Dyson and Featherstone 1996b: 342). It is important, therefore, to explore the following three points:

- Why did European policy makers agree upon the desirability of this paradigm of central bank independence? This yields an examination of the process of cognitive convergence, which took place throughout the 1980s.
- What does the paradigm embraced at Maastricht consist of (and whether there were alternative paradigms)?
- Which interests were better served by the paradigm chosen at Maastricht? This last point will function as a conceptual bridge between the analysis of the cognitive component of the policy process and the analysis of actors.

The 1980s were a decade of radical reorientation of policy-makers' beliefs about the conduct of macro-economic policy, in the EU and elsewhere (Hall 1986; 1989; McNamara 1998). Countries such as France and Italy learned that traditional Keynesian policies based on deficit spending and generous welfare state provisions were no longer feasible. Even socialist governments (in France, but also, outside Europe, in Australia and New Zealand) had to come to terms with the new orthodoxy of sound finance and price stability. The control of inflation became the prime goal of macro-economic policy, more important than fighting unemployment. France presents the paradigmatic example. The Mitterrand government, elected in 1981, sought to respond to a recession by relying on traditional Keynesian policies. The attempt to reflate the economy by using macro-economic policy, however, triggered inflation and trade deficit. Additionally, capital left the country and the franc was subject to intensive speculative attacks. The French government discovered that the only way out of this uncomfortable economic condition was to pursue a rigorous disinflationary policy, bringing France's main indicators (inflation and interest rates) in line with those of Germany.

Parallel to this cognitive reorientation of the French government, there has been, since 1982–83, a process of institutionalization of Franco-German policy coordination. This process has comprised of both formal acts, such as the Franco-German economic Council (since 1988) and a series of secret meetings paralleling the intergovernmental conference on EMU (Dyson and Featherstone 1996b). This process, among other things, made the policy beliefs of German and French policy makers preparing EMU more similar than they were at the beginning of the 1980s. In short, France (and with it other European countries) came closer to embracing the typical ordo-liberal economic orthodoxy of Germany. Ordo-liberalism doctrine – as illustrated by Dyson and Featherstone (1996b: 334) – posits that the main economic function of the state is to provide price stability; that in order to deliver on price stability, monetary policy has to be depoliticized (that is, central bank independence); and that a culture of stability, responsible moderation and macro-economic compatibility has to be shared by all economic agents, from the government to trade unions, firms and citizens.

In 1988, when countries such as Italy and France agreed to the proposal of liberalizing capital movement and sustained the idea of an independent central bank for EMU, the process of cognitive convergence had made considerable progress. This had two effects. On the one hand, German policy makers appreciated the fundamental shift in French policy. Dyson and Featherstone (1996b: 335) refer to a 'restructuring of German economic policy arguments', meaning a growing perception, among German policy makers, that a deal with France might be feasible because France would accept an EMU based on sound money, sound prices and sound finance. On the other, the convergence of economic policy beliefs made the adoption of key decisions about the structure of the single currency less controversial than it might have been otherwise. As averred, German policy makers and bankers did not have to go out of their way to persuade their European partners of the need to mould the European Central Bank along the model of the Bundesbank. The partners had already learnt this lesson at home.

What was the lesson learnt throughout the 1980s? Plainly, that modern economies could not exploit a trade-off between inflation and unemployment.[37] Prior to the 1980s, the conventional wisdom was that policy makers could make a choice between the alternative goals of price stability and employment. They could either pursue a price stability strategy, at the cost of aggravating the situation of the labour market, or promote employment, but with a cost in terms of inflation. However, if expectations are introduced in the trade-off between inflation and employment, the relation does not hold anymore (Friedman 1968; Phelps 1968). For economic agents expecting the government to push the economy via inflationary deficit spending will immediately include the new level of inflation in their expectations. This will influence their behaviour. For example, they will negotiate salaries with a higher inflation rate already in mind. Inflation will then rise before an increase in real variables (output and employment) materializes. Accordingly, there will be a unique unemployment rate compatible with the equilibrium of the economy, and no government effort to pump up the economy will result in anything else than inflation. This is what economists mean when they talk about a 'natural' rate of unemployment. Given this situation, the government should not attempt to cheat in front of economic agents with rational expectations: the best economic policy strategy is commitment to price stability.[38]

A policy of low inflation is therefore best in the long run. All the same, governments have political incentives to deviate from this policy in the short run (Barro and Gordon 1983). They can be either lobbied by firms asking for easy credit, or court the electorate because they need votes. If governments do so, they will boost the economy before elections, knowing that the economic costs of this decision will become evident only after elections. In sum, governments can reap the benefits of short-term increased spending, win elections, and then face difficult economic times during the post-election honeymoon, where the voters are no longer threatening the incumbent. These propositions, known as the political business cycle model (Lewis-Beck 1988), have an important political implication. Elected politicians should not be given the opportunity to manipulate the money supply. This is tantamount to saying that monetary policy should be entrusted to an independent central bank (Alesina 1989).

How can a price stability strategy be made feasible? The crucial element – from the point of view of the government – is reputation. If economic actors do not believe in the government's commitment to low inflation, their expectations for high inflation will be reflected in their decisions about wages and prices, and this will yield high inflation. Reputation, however, is not a resource that can be easily made available. The Bundesbank has built up its reputation as a credible monetary institution in the course of a long history of harsh decisions, and a long series of 'no' to politicians and firms demanding inflationary boosts. Countries where monetary policy has been traditionally lax cannot utilize their past history to make themselves credible. Yet they can borrow credibility from institutions such as the Bundesbank by 'tying their hands' to the Deutschmark, to German interests rates, and ultimately to the monetary policy of the most credible monetary institution in Europe (Giavazzi and Pagano 1988).

Central bank independence and the 'tying one's hands' strategy are the two crucial ingredients of the EMU policy design. A third ingredient is a series of constraints, from the 'no bail out' rules chosen at Maastricht to the more recent stability pact (Eichengreen and Wyplosz 1998; Hahn 1998) ensuring that, once in full operation, the EMU policy regime will re-create at the EU level the German monetary regime. In this respect, economic policy paradigms have been extremely important in shaping EMU. It should be noted, however, that the paradigm of central bank independence and 'tying one's hands' has not been uncontested among economists. For one reason, certain economists believe that the competition among currencies is efficient, and should not be disposed of easily. Those economists are hostile to the idea of constraining the market in any form. For another, the above mentioned school of optimum currency areas has a more respectable 'pedigree' than credibility – political business cycle models. It should be kept in mind that the conclusion of the theory of optimum currency areas is that the EU as a monetary union has more chances of failing than succeeding. As Dyson (1994: 247) puts it:

> Though credibility theory and the theory of the political business cycle has captured the EMS and EMU policy process, the main axis of debate about monetary unions in international monetary economics remained the theory of optimum currency areas. The EMS and EMU policy process was unable to avoid confrontation with the theoretical and practical implications of the fact that the EC did not constitute an optimum currency area.

He continues with the observation that 'even the thesis that central bank independence explained low inflation was challenged. There was evidence to suggest that the nature of the institutions of the labour market was at least as important as central bank independence in affecting the rate of inflation' (Dyson 1994: 248). Remember, in fact, that the ordo-liberal model is not limited to monetary policy design. It also hinges on a culture of stability permeating the behaviour of trade unions, firms, and citizens. This was a fundamental component of the German success in keeping inflation low throughout the 1980s.

Moreover, there are reasons to believe that EMU will find it difficult to re-establish the German policy regime at the EU level. There are incentives to free ride in the third stage of EMU. For example, a large country such as Italy could exploit EMU membership by running a considerable deficit in the expectation that the Italian economy is too big to fail.[39] Like in Goethe's Faust, Italy could commit the sin of fiscal profligacy knowing that Margarita (the rest of EMU countries) will ultimately save her.[40] In addition, the decision to fine a country must be taken by a qualified majority in the Council of Ministers, and it is not inconceivable to hypothesize that a coalition of high-expenditure countries could outvote Germany (Garrett 1993: 111). For these reasons, the EMU design has been strengthened by the stability pact. The latter, however, is bound to create a negative demand shock in the early years of EMU, with European unemployment already at a daunting 12 per cent level. Hence the argument that EMU will yield German economic virtues writ large is far from being indisputable.

The policy paradigm enshrined in EMU presents more than one problem.[41] However, the fact that the model is flawed or could work less efficiently than imagined at Maastricht does not alter its importance. Flawed or not, this is the model around which the whole EMU design revolves. Why then was it accepted without strong opposition? The process of cognitive convergence described above tells us part of the story. Another part is told by the preferences which were better served at the table of Maastricht. As the old Romans asked, *cui bono,* in the interest of whom?[42] The Treaty of Maastricht, although not impeccable in its economic underpinnings, fits in nicely with the interests of central bankers, who were empowered by the decisions regarding central bank independence and sound finance. It also appealed to savers, who are the most important constituency to gain from a world of low inflation, and to monetary policy experts in finance ministries and within the Commission (Dyson and Featherstone 1996a; 1999). But, essentially, the most striking feature of EMU is the amount of power it assigns to central bankers. The Commission had desired a larger role for itself and the European Parliament in the policy process, but it lost. Equally, the French negotiators insisted on a *gouvernement economique* to counterbalance the power of the European Central Bank without success. The splendid isolation of the European Central Bank as the leading actor in core EMU decisions is the most evident success achieved by central bankers. This stimulates an analysis of EMU in terms of actors, rather than ideas and economic policy paradigms. It is to this type of analysis that we now turn.

Bankers as actors in the EMU policy process

The EU policy process is characterized by its fluidity. A large number of institutional actors, pressure groups, and expert committees flesh out the design of EU public policies. There is no clear centre of gravity, such as the cabinet in the British political system, or the parliament in certain European countries. However, the EMU policy process constitutes a major deviation from this pattern. For EMU was concocted and designed within a relatively isolated policy milieu, 'composed of central bankers (in the EC's Committee of Central Bank Governors); finance ministers and their officials (in ECOFIN); and finance ministry officials and their central bank equivalents (in the EC's Monetary Committee)' (Dyson and Featherstone 1997: 10).

Dyson and Featherstone (1997: 9) remind us that even within the Commission, the Commission's submission to the intergovernmental conference was discussed 'in the most limited manner'. More often than not, when it comes to setting the agenda of EU public policy the Commission resembles a political system. Different DGs and commissioners conflict over draft directives, the competence of the Commission in certain areas, and the interpretation of key events, as will be illustrated by media ownership policy in Chapter Six. But in the case of EMU the then president of the Commission, Jacques Delors, maintained a firm grip on the whole Commission. Moreover, he chaired the Delors Committee. We have already observed the influence of this Committee. The Delors Committee is yet another example of the isolated policy milieu characterizing EMU. Composed of twelve central bank governors, three independent figures and a chair, it was set up, as seen above, by the Hanover European Council in June 1988.

As averred, the EMU design can be questioned from the standpoint of economic theory. All the same, it is consistent with the preferences of central bank governors. The question arises whether technocracy was at work in the EMU policy process in the form of a key role played by central bankers. The Delors Committee is an obvious candidate for supporting this hypothesis. To avoid confusion, however, a distinction between economists and central bankers should be maintained throughout the analysis. What we are looking for is evidence of the key role of central bankers. Economists were (and are) divided over the costs and benefits of EMU, the best conceptual approach (optimum currency areas or credibility *cum* political business cycle), and the timing of the three stages. Therefore the question to be considered concerns central bankers alone.

Two studies[43] (Cameron 1995; Verdun 1997) have been presented with the aim of addressing our question, although they pursue different aims. Cameron examined central bankers as actors of transnational politics, that is, 'a type of politics that involved neither the national governments of the member states nor actors embedded in the supranational institutions of the Community' (Cameron 1995: 73). His account suggests that:

> Transnational actors and their politics were present and influential *throughout* the development of the EMU initiative, from the first meetings of the Delors Committee in 1988 to the last meetings of the inter-governmental conference nearly four years later, and in some respects and at some moments, they were *more* influential than *either* governmental or supranational actors.
>
> (Cameron 1995: 73–4, emphasis in original)

Not only – he argues – was the Delors Committee instrumental in transforming the political commitment of the Hanover summit into a feasible project from EMU, but even draft treaties submitted to the intergovernmental conference were first scrutinized by the central bankers community and then discussed on a more political level. Cameron also makes the point that the crucial documents such as the Dutch draft treaty acquired legitimacy in the eyes of policy makers precisely because they had been prepared in close consultation with central bankers.

Verdun (1997) asserts that the Delors Committee matches the definition of an epistemic community provided by Haas (as reviewed in Chapter Three). She argues that the concept of epistemic community is appropriate in the first instance as it draws attention to a small network of individuals working in a highly institutionalized policy environment (the European Community and the institutions of international monetary policy), thus avoiding the broader scientific community. The latter – as already seen – was divided and often distant from the making of EMU. According to Verdun, the Committee fulfils the following criteria provided by the definition of epistemic community. The Committee shared a set of normative and principled beliefs, such as the belief that European monetary integration, under certain conditions of economic convergence, would be desirable. They also shared causal beliefs, as indicated by the focus of the Committee on the paradigm of central bank independence, reputation and policy credibility. Finally, the members of the Delors Committee were involved in a common policy enterprise. Indeed, they were selected with the aim of sustaining a precise policy enterprise with their input.

Much of the work done by Verdun deals eminently with the correspondence between the Delors Committee and the definitional characteristics of epistemic community. Verdun, additionally, makes two important points when she argues that (a) the Delors Committee was not a sort of apolitical actor which stood above politics and (b) the Committee was asked for advice (that is, how to create EMU) by national decision makers in search of legitimacy and knowledge.[44] It is precisely the link between the Committee and its political environment that needs more exploration. Indeed, to reiterate a point made in Chapter Three, 'epistemic communities create realities, but not as they wish' (Adler and Haas 1992: 381). It is important to establish – as Verdun and Cameron do – the influence of the Delors Committee in setting the EMU design, although it is essential to look at the broader political forces at work prior to Hanover and during the intergovernmental conference. In the next section we will turn to this issue again, drawing upon the distinction between technical feasibility and political acceptability. But in any case one should bear in mind that the Delors Committee was established as a consequence of a clear (yet secret) strategic initiative between the French government, the German foreign ministry, Kohl and Delors. They took the political decisions to go ahead with EMU plans, thus marginalizing the British government.[45]

In this respect, the Delors Committee was a perfect tool for a sophisticated political strategy. It was an instrument through which a reluctant Bundesbank was locked in the EMU policy process. 'Its composition' – Dyson and Featherstone (1996b: 345) report – 'infuriated Pöhl who recognised its real intent: to bind the Bundesbank *de facto* into the process of designing EMU and rid it of the opportunity to criticise proposals from the sidelines'. Thus the role of what might as well have been an epistemic community was severely constrained by broader political forces, operating within the Commission and the governments of France and Germany.

But was the Delors Committee in actual fact an epistemic community? Typically, epistemic communities operate in areas where the degree of uncertainty is so high that policy makers have to rely on experts even for understanding their real interests. Think of extremely complex areas of environmental policy or health policy, where only scientists can detect whether there is causation between a certain chemical element and pollution or a specific disease. However, in the case of EMU the process of cognitive convergence illustrated above shows that policy makers came to agree on a set of economic principles (such as policy credibility) for the design of monetary policy. When they sat together, experts did not have to convince policy makers on the issue of tight monetary policy or the benefits of reputation in terms of low inflation. Policy makers had already been convinced by the radical failure of traditional policies in the 1970s and early 1980s. True, differences remained between countries (obviously France held a different view of EU monetary policy to the British government) and within governments, as shown by the different opinions in the German government. But these conflicts were genuinely political, rather than being issues of uncertainty where the enlightening function of experts could be displayed. To conclude on this point, it is hard to argue that policy makers were puzzling over radical uncertainty and that an epistemic community offered an interpretation of a complex reality, thus contributing to the definition of member states' preferences. Policy makers knew what their preferences were and asked the Delors Committee for an operationalization of those preferences.

In addition, most of the bankers within the Delors Committee – although formally sitting in the committee in their personal capacity – were not that independent from their government, a point which both Cameron and Verdun concede. Indeed, for countries with a tradition of central bank independence such as Germany it was just physiologic to have a certain dialectic confrontation between central bankers and governments. For other countries, where central banks were much less independent, the common pattern was one of alignment of the central bank's position to the governmental position. If independence is an important prerequisite for autonomous behaviour, then it should be said that not all the members of the Delors Committee possessed this prerequisite.

Finally, the Delors Committee was chaired by the president of the Commission, not by a central banker. Although Delors had experience in the world of international monetary policy as former Minister of Finance in France, and therefore should not be considered alien to the other components of the Committee, he was also the entrepreneurial head of a powerful European institution. Delors was seeking an opportunity to relaunch monetary union, a long-standing goal of the Commission, and he played his role within the Committee according to his strategy of empowering the Commission through EMU. So much so that there were several episodes of confrontation between Delors and the other members of the Committee.

More importantly still, Delors was the advocate of a specific 'policy frame of reference' which can hardly be defined the frame of a rather neutral expert. As illustrated by Dyson and Featherstone (1997: 17, emphasis in original), his policy frame was highly political as it comprised of, *inter alia*, 'the priority to be given to institutions to lead integration and change patterns of behaviour; and the recognition that EMU was, ultimately, a *political* project – to advance the European cause – rather than merely a question of economics. It thus needed a firm political lead and commitment, preferably with a clearly defined timetable'. Indeed, the very appointment of Delors as chair of the Committee 'ensured a strong political lead in favour of further integration. The Committee was thus carefully crafted to achieve the essential objective of Delors and Kohl' (Dyson and Featherstone 1997: 18).

The Delors Committee was more than a technical exercise, although it was deliberately presented as such in order to avoid ruffling British feathers at the Hanover summit. The political dimension of the Committee became apparent also in key meetings, such as the tense confrontation between monetarists and institutionalists at the March 1989 meeting (Cameron 1995: 48). In conclusion, the internal fragmentation of the Committee, the broader political project which it served, and the presence of a chair with a political strategy do not provide fully convincing evidence of an epistemic community at work under EMU.

A technocratic EMU?

The EMU policy process up until Maastricht is indicative of the political power of expertise. EMU was fleshed out in an isolated policy milieu, its design chimes with the preferences of central bankers and monetary technocrats, and the crucial components of the path to the single currency were chosen by a supposedly technical committee, the Delors Committee.

As explained in Chapter Three, expertise can secure legitimacy by dint of three mechanisms of policy diffusion (that is, mimetism, coercion and normative pressures). As averred, these mechanisms can provide technocratic legitimacy, limited to the success of policy within the institutional perimeter of the EU, whereas democratic legitimacy is a wider concept, covering the consensus of citizens. Having clarified this, how did the mechanisms of policy diffusion operate in the case of the single currency? Firstly, the diffusion of the policy credibility model was possible because the EMU policy process had a clear centre of gravity, represented by the Deutschmark. Thus a certain degree of *coercive* diffusion can be detected in terms of the anchor power of the Deutschmark. Secondly, not only was the Deutschmark a centripetal force in the EMU policy process, but the whole institutional set-up of German monetary policy appeared a good example to be imitated and transferred into the Treaty of Maastricht. The pervasive presence of the policy credibility paradigm in the EMU policy process is the result of *mimetism*: at Maastricht, uncertainty found a response in the imitation of the (perceived) most successful national model of monetary policy. Mimetic isomorphism secured legitimacy during this stage of the EMU policy process. Thirdly, perhaps a case can be made for *normative* pressure too, when considering to what extent the Delors Committee was instrumental in shaping the EMU policy process in accordance with the shared beliefs and values of the central bankers profession.

The fact that limited, *technocratic legitimacy* was the crucial element in this episode of policy transfer was demonstrated by the fragility of the EMU success. EU policy transfer is inherently vulnerable in terms of *democratic legitimacy*. In the case of EMU, the politics of expertise had completely overlooked the cultural dimension of money (Dyson 1994). As soon as 1992, the road to monetary union became rough and steep (Sandholtz 1996), and even the recent success of the eleven countries giving birth to the Euro (May 1998) has not deterred many European citizens from their scepticism about the single currency. Isomorphism, learning and economic policy paradigms secured technocratic legitimacy at the Maastricht table. But the other side of legitimacy, that is, widespread democratic consensus, remains the major challenge for EMU: it is indeed the very Damocles' sword hanging over the completion of the single currency project. European institutions, most notably the Commission, are currently at pains to show EU citizens that the single currency is part and parcel of European citizenship.

A final remark on coercion. The effort to respect the convergence criteria and qualify for the single currency has now produced in countries such as France, Germany, Italy and Spain a coercion to restructure public finance and reform the welfare state. 'When the Maastricht Treaty was *drafted*' – Bovenberg and de Jong note – 'the criteria did not seem too stringent.' (Bovenberg and de Jong 1997: 94, emphasis added). However, afterwards it became more difficult to be in line with the convergence criteria and for the future the stability pact will make the path of economic policy within the Euro-zone even narrower. During the years, the coercive aspects of EMU have gained importance, so much so that they are now prevailing over mimetism.

Concluding on this point, mechanisms of technocratic legitimacy were important features of the EMU policy process. All the same, the political elements surrounding policy experts should not be overlooked. At key junctures, EMU was steered by political forces, especially the Franco-German axis. The Commission with its entrepreneurial leader, Jacques Delors, was also one of the EMU *animateurs* and strategists, although it was more instrumental in setting the agenda and creating momentum for EMU than in the final negotiations which took place at Maastricht. In the end, it was a political calculation in terms of German re-unification that prodded Kohl at the EMU deal at Maastricht, thus distancing himself from the cautious and occasionally sceptical position of the Bundesbank.

My conclusion is that political decision making mattered, and ultimately prevailed over the politics of expertise. In terms of the typology introduced in Chapter Three, the political power of expertise can take the forms of bureaucratic politics, technocracy or epistemic communities (see Figure 3.2 in Chapter Three, p. 48). On balance, the power of expertise in EMU is better captured by the category of epistemic community, rather than bureaucratic politics or technocracy. However, the Delors Committee does not fulfil completely the conceptual coordinates of the epistemic community model for the reasons outlined above. More importantly still, political decision making prevailed over the political power of expertise. This conclusion can be clarified by considering the difference between technical feasibility and political acceptability.[46] The politics of expertise (especially epistemic communities) should be assigned a premium insofar as it concerns the *technical feasibility* of EMU. This is the domain where the preferences of central bankers[47] were incorporated in the Treaty. More generally, the whole cognitive dimension of EMU was permeated by shared beliefs about central bank independence and policy credibility which (a) originated with the failure of Keynesian economic policies; (b) were sustained by a particular version of monetarism; and (c) found in German monetary policy an existing, desirable example to be imitated (McNamara 1998). This ideational dimension of EMU was strengthened by the role played by the Delors Committee. The ideational dimension of EMU (that is, its technical feasibility) exhibits a strong influence of epistemic communities, although the previous reservations on the extent to which the Delors Committee should be considered an epistemic community apply. However, there was another dimension of the EMU policy process concerning its *political acceptability*. Our analysis suggests that the cognitive dimension of politics was accompanied by an intense strategic activity made of network building,[48] political opportunities,[49] and even secret negotiations.[50] It was this eminently political dimension to define the boundaries of what was politically acceptable and, ultimately, to transform a set of ideas into a treaty.

Notes

1   Known to the layman as the Maastricht Treaty.
2   Nominal is opposed to real convergence, that is, convergence in terms of output and employment.
3   Under article 104c of the Treaty, governments with 'excessive deficits' may be fined or required to maintain zero-interest deposits in the European Central Bank.
4   Dyson (1994) draws attention to the structural power of the Deutschmark as anchor currency in Europe, but also to the power of financial markets.
5   Think of the impact of German re-unification upon the behaviour of Chancellor Kohl during the negotiations leading up to the Maastricht

Treaty. Many studies address the issue of Maastricht and domestic politics. Sandholtz (1993) investigates the construction of national preferences, Martin (1993) examines issue-linkages and the role of domestic institutions, Garrett (1993) and Dyson and Featherstone (1996b) analyse the domestic and foreign policy preferences of Germany. McNamara (1998) looks at how the interplay between the change in economic structure (that is, the growth of capital mobility) and domestic policy choices. Her idea is that a neo-liberal policy consensus emerged across Europe in the 1970s, following the failure of traditional Keynesian policies, the rise of monetarism, and the emulation of German monetary policy. Finally, Dyson (1994), drawing upon Putnam (1988), presents a model of bargaining based on two levels, that is, domestic politics and EU politics.

6 For these models the reader should refer to Garrett (1993), Dyson (1994), Dyson and Featherstone (1999), Martin (1993), McNamara (1998), and Sandholtz (1993). Eichengreen (1997), although not concerned with the politics of Maastricht as his main analytic goal, provides an excellent politico-economic assessment of EMU. Cameron (1995) does not present a model, yet he provides a concise narrative of the events culminating at Maastricht.

7 Amy Verdun raised this point in a personal communication (4 September 1998). She invited me to make it clear that I am not contrasting politics with supposedly apolitical forms of public policy making, but different forms of political power.

8 On the relationship between currency fluctuations and the administration of the Common Agricultural Policy see McNamara (1998: Chapter 5).

9 On the birth of EMU as a Community goal and the proposals aired between the end of the 1960s and the Werner plan (1970) see Tsoukalis (1977).

10 Barre's argument – Dyson (1994: 72) sums up – was that the Community 'had to respond to a new source of structural power: namely that the customs union and the CAP had produced such a degree of economic interdependence among the member states that national economic policy decisions could no longer be effective if taken in isolation'.

11 These are the words appearing in the final *communiqué*.

12 It should be observed that the label 'monetarist' refers to a particular position in the EMU debate. It should not be confused with the wider monetarist school of economic thought originated by Milton Friedman and his acolytes.

13 Germany was afraid that, in the absence of economic policy coordination, the Bundesbank reserves would have to be employed to sustain weak European currencies.

14 See Rosenthal (1975) and Tsoukalis (1977). Speaking to the press, the then Italian finance minister, Emilio Colombo, stated that 'the unification of economic policy implies an acceleration of the process of economic integration. It is becoming more and more apparent in these discussions that monetary cooperation aimed at the eventual adoption of a common currency is impossible if economic policies lack not only coordination but unification as well' (quoted by Rosenthal 1975: 103–4).

15 Rosenthal contrasted five case studies. She found that EMU was the case where the influence of the elite network was most intense.

16 On the continuity between the snake and the EMS see Dyson (1994: Chapter Four).

17 The Exchange Rate Mechanism allowed realignments and provided financial facilities for countries facing episodic balance of payments shocks. In short, it was a system wherein exchange rates were pegged yet adjustable. On the EMS negotiations see Ludlow (1982).

18 Fratianni and von Hagen (1991) provide a comprehensive assessment of the EMS.

19 It should be observed, however, that there was a rationale for the asymmetrical nature of the EMS. As shown by Giavazzi and Pagano (1988), the asymmetric EMS acted as a disciplinary device. Countries with low credibility in fighting inflation would be forced to follow the Bundesbank's monetary policy by pegging their exchange rates to the strongest currency within the EMS, that is, the Deutschmark. By following the Bundesbank, European countries would 'borrow' its reputation as an institution committed to price stability. Thus the asymmetry of the EMS would be the price to pay for gaining reputation and in turn low inflation in Europe.

20 E. Balladur, 'Europe's monetary construction', Memorandum to ECOFIN Council, Paris, 8 January 1988.

21 Bluntly, Balladur's strategy could be summarized by the proposition that 'a greater voice in EMU would be preferable to continued German dominance in the EMS' (Sandholtz 1993: 30).

22 G. Amato, 'Un motore per lo SME', Il Sole-24Ore, 25 February 1988.

23 Tommaso Padoa-Schioppa, from 1979 to 1983 Director General of DG2 (economic and financial affairs) of the Commission, chaired a group of experts who produced the report. See Padoa-Schioppa (1988; 1994).

24 Its official name was Committee for the Study of Economic and Monetary Union.

25 Committee for the Study of Economic and Monetary Union (1989) *Report on Economic and Monetary Union in the European Community* (Delors Report), Luxembourg, European Communities.

26 A second intergovernmental conference took place, dedicated to the political union.

27 The European Monetary Institute was entrusted with the task of doing the preparatory work before stage three.

28 This was to become the so-called principle of irreversibility of EMU.

29 However, the Delors Report (CSEMU 1989: 16) recognized that EMU would represent 'a quantum jump' and not an automatic consequence of the single market.

30 See Eichengreen and Frieden (1993) and the studies mentioned in their paper.

31 Calculated on the then twelve members EU which existed during the negotiations of the Maastricht Treaty. See Eichengreen and Frieden (1993: 90).

32 See the classic Mundell (1961) and Eichengreen (1997).

33 Put differently, the second prerequisite is the presence of a system of fiscal federalism. In their study of how the stabilization mechanisms of fiscal federalism operate in the USA, Sala-i-Martin and Sachs (1992) have estimated that a one dollar reduction in a USA region's per-capita income triggers a decrease in federal taxes of about thirty-four cents, and an increase in federal transfers of about six cents.

34 It must be stressed that the exchange rate is an adequate instrument for certain types of shocks, that is, shocks which are temporary, real (as opposed to monetary), and country-specific.

35 Studies of existing monetary unions have raised doubts as to whether even federal countries such as Canada and the USA fulfil the criteria of optimum currency area models completely. Yet these countries are closer to the ideal of an optimum currency area than the EU.

36 Sound money because of the tight rules for the conduct of monetary policy, sound inflation because of the overriding commitment to price stability, and sound finance because of the stringent limits on public deficits and debts.

37 The trade-off is illustrated by the Phillips curve (Phillips 1958). Interestingly, the Phillips curve stems for a long-term analysis of wages and prices, but is not well grounded in an economic theory or model. It is more a statistical correlation than an economic explanation and it is surprising to observe for how long it has been believed by policy makers.

38 Not all economists believe in this series of causal relationships, but it is safe to state that the majority of economists (belonging to different strands of neoclassical economics) certainly do.

39 See Garrett (1993) for this logic.

40 Interestingly, this is precisely what former central banker and Italian minister Guido Carli (1993) feared.

41 De Grauwe has consistently exposed the limitations of this paradigm. See De Grauwe (1992; 1994; 1996).

42 Here I draw upon Dyson (1994: 235).

43 One should also remember that Rosenthal (1975) found evidence of a small network elite at the centre of the first EMU design (the one contained in the Werner Report). It would follow that there has always been a technocratic bias in European monetary policy.

44 These two points are very clear in the most recent re-presentation of her argument (Verdun 1998).

45 Dyson and Featherstone (1997: 13) explain that the deal leading to the establishment of the Delors Committee 'had been a carefully crafted deal, kept secret from most, if not all, the rest. Thatcher was caught unaware'.

46 I borrow the two terms, that is, technical feasibility and political acceptability, from Dyson and Featherstone (1998).

47 And technocratic experts working in finance ministries, as explained by Dyson and Featherstone (1996a).

48 Think of the relationship between the German and French foreign ministries for an example. Another example is the construction of a coalition of monetarists–institutionalists and the breakdown of the economists' front (with Spain defecting) following the decisions taken at Ashford Castle.

49 German re-unification, presumably, was the greatest political opportunity sustaining the EMU deal at Maastricht. Another political opportunity was represented by the possibility to lock-in the Bundesbank in the EMU policy process by setting up the Delors Committee.

50 For example, the British government was not made aware of the strategic implications of the establishment of the Delors Committee. Further, the institutionalization of Franco-German relations was buttressed by a series of secret bilateral discussions during the intergovernmental conference.

CHAPTER FIVE

Tax policy in the European Union: technocracy or politicization?

Direct tax policy is a neglected – yet fundamental – component of the single market. For one reason, certain taxes can create serious distortions in the single market. Instead of a level playing field, citizens and companies end up facing discriminatory taxes, residents are taxed differently from non-residents, tax benefits are lost to workers who live in one country and work in another, free trade is impeded by double taxation of cross-border income flows, and the growth of genuine European multinationals is hindered.

For another, under certain conditions tax competition[1] can trigger perverse dynamics. When this happens, it is the collective welfare of the community that suffers. Tax rates on mobile factors are set to sub-optimal levels, and companies do not invest where efficiency is higher but where taxes are lower. Capital, therefore, is inefficiently allocated. This happens if countries compete aggressively by offering no or low taxes to foreign capital, bank secrecy, generous tax expenditures for foreign companies, and lack of collaboration with foreign tax authorities. Not only does harmful tax competition jeopardize the single market it can also shake the fundament of the European welfare state. The welfare state is predestined to a grinding halt if capital does not provide its fair share of revenue, with the less mobile workers[2] bearing the weight of financing social programmes.

The tabloid version of harmful tax competition paints an unlikely picture of wealthy *individuals* investing their savings abroad. Indeed, there has been much speculation in the non-specialist press about trains full of Belgian pensioners who leave Brussels on Monday morning, go to Luxembourg with their savings, and come back after banking over lunch in the fairy-tale Grand Duchy, well known for the favourable treatment of non-resident savers. However, the big players in the tax competition game are sophisticated *multi-national enterprises* moving head offices and other non-locational services to special tax regimes, or shifting income between parents and subsidiaries in such a way as to concentrate profits where tax rates are low and costs where rates are high. Offshore banking centres, captive insurance companies and aggressive financial intermediaries complete the team of players. Hence, contrary to conventional wisdom, corporate taxation is probably at least as important as the taxation of individual portfolios.

Taxation is certainly a technical issue. International taxation is perhaps the most complicated and technical of all tax policies. The main problems caused by international taxation in the single market are double taxation, discrimination against non-resident workers, and the undesirable effects of tax competition. There are several channels through which taxes levied in one member state affect the welfare of other member states, thus creating international spillover effects. If a company, as already shown, shifts income through tax planning and makes profits appear in countries with low statutory tax rates, a revenue loss has been imposed by the low rate country on the high rate country. In this example there is no shifting of real economic activity. But the mobility of the tax base is a sufficient condition for allocating revenue losses in another country. Another example is the existence of taxes on the return of foreign-owned capital. Let us assume that a government levies a withholding tax on dividends paid to non-residents. By doing so, this government will export part of its tax burden, and thereby will impose a welfare loss on a foreign country. A final example is when a company is taxed in a foreign country on its profits. It may happen that the payment of taxes abroad is not acknowledged in full by the company's country of residence. This is a case of double taxation that creates a disincentive to the growth of European multinationals. When international double taxation exists, a company has no incentive to invest abroad.

To introduce order in this complexity, it is necessary to take into account the three main features of corporate taxes: the system chosen for the taxation of profits, the rates, and the fiscal base (for instance, the ways in which income and profits are defined for fiscal reasons). Systems differ according to the presence (in which case there is an imputation system) or absence (in which case the system is dubbed classic) of an integration between the fiscal treatment of corporate profits and the fiscal treatment for the shareholder of dividends paid out of those profits. A third system – for example, the so-called split-rate – has been chosen by countries where there is no link between corporation tax and income tax, but nevertheless distributed profits are treated differently from non-distributed ones.

The system chosen for the taxation of profits, the rates and the tax base are three important sources of variation in the single market. Of course, most of this variation corresponds to legitimately different options pursued by governments and electorates with dissimilar objectives. However, there are circumstances where tax differences originate discrimination, double taxation and harmful tax competition. It is therefore not surprising to observe that the argument for European tax coordination was made a long time ago.

Given the complexity of international tax policy, one would expect a typical pattern of technocratic policy making. From the point of view of the Commission, couching tax policy in a technocratic policy process has the great advantage of smothering down the political anxieties of member states. Taxation is in fact a bulwark of the nation state, and no government is keen on the idea of severing the political-electoral link between taxation, representation, and welfare programmes. This is why member states have conceded a certain amount of power to European institutions in indirect taxes, whilst direct taxes have remained a more or less intact preserve of domestic decisions. A certain degree of indirect tax harmonization has been perceived as essential for the free movement of *goods* (and hence a number of directives on value added taxes and excise duties have been adopted throughout the years). However, the thorny question of direct tax distortions affecting the behaviour of *companies* and the freedom of the *individual* (simply put, direct tax coordination) has been dealt with much less successfully. Obviously, the two goals of free movement of goods and a single market for labour, businesses and capital involve political difficulties of enormously different magnitude. Technocratic policy making appears a prima facie solution to the problem of getting around the stiff political opposition of member states to European level coordination of direct taxes.

This chapter will therefore examine the development of the EU direct tax policy process,[3] with particular emphasis on corporate taxation, and seek to respond to the following questions:

- To what extent does technocracy represent a major characteristic of the EU direct tax policy process?
- What are the major arguments used in tax policy? Do they point towards technical considerations (for example, taxation as a means to achieve efficiency) or toward the political determination needed to coordinate taxes in the EU?
- If technocracy is present, has the Commission sought to promote the growth of EU tax policy via technocratic policy making? Arguably, one should expect the Commission to press for a technocratic discourse, and member states stressing the political components of tax coordination.

The answer will be mixed, with the Commission insisting on a technocratic approach to tax policy only in one particular period. Recent events, however, show that the Commission has shunned a technocratic approach to tax policy. Indeed, since 1995 the Commission has been one of most active actors in advocating for a more political definition of tax issues. How has it been possible? It is to this question that we now turn, by examining the earlier attempts to tax harmonization, the technocratic phase, and the more recent political stage of the EU direct tax policy process.

The earlier attempts

The Treaties provide very limited legal resources for EU direct tax policy. The Treaty of Rome contains specific provisions for indirect taxation (Articles 95–9), but in direct taxation only Article 100[4] and Article 220 can be employed. In particular, Article 220 has a definitively intergovernmental nature, for it stipulates that 'Member states shall, so far as is necessary, enter into negotiations with each other with a view to securing for the benefit of their nationals: ... the abolition of double taxation within the Community'. Unanimity at the Council level is required,[5] and the Treaties of Maastricht and Amsterdam[6] have not modified the voting system.

However, important general principles are laid down in Article 48 (free movement of people), Article 52 (freedom of establishment), Article 59 (free provision of services), and Article 67 (free movement of capital). Although they do not refer to tax policy specifically, they set the perimeter of the single market that has to be buttressed by consistent tax measures. The European Court of

Justice, additionally, can make use of these principles for striking down national rules. Article 73 – as modified by the Treaty on the European Union – has a more questionable meaning. On the one hand, Article 73b (now Article 56 in the consolidated version of the treaties) inserted by the Treaty of Maastricht, prohibits all restrictions on the movement of capital in the single market. But the same Treaty inserted a more contentious article, 73d (Article 58 in the consolidated version). The latter does not prejudice 'the right of member states to apply the relevant provisions of their tax law which distinguish between taxpayers who are not in the same situation with regard to their place of residence or with regard to the place where their capital is invested'. The same article, however, sets the following limitation: 'the measures and procedures ... shall not constitute a means of arbitrary discrimination or a disguised restriction on the free movement of capital'. The result is that national tax rules placing a disadvantage on inward investment from, or outward investment to, another member state are not prohibited explicitly, provided that they are not discriminatory.[7] Although the article does not provide a defence for discriminatory tax rules, it allows member states to retain non-discriminatory restrictions in their tax systems, such as withholding taxes on intra-community interest and royalty payments and the denial of tax credits to foreign shareholders under imputation systems.

This limited treaty base did not prevent the Commission from making proposals for direct tax policy coordination. The distortionary influence of domestic tax measures on the establishment and functioning of the common market was recognized soon after the conclusion of the European Economic Community Treaty (that is, the Treaty of Rome). On 5 April 1960 the Commission set up a Fiscal and Financial Committee chaired by Professor Fritz Neumark. The Committee delivered a report in July 1962. At that time the most important problem of the common market was the free movement of goods and the establishment of a customs union, and understandably most of the attention of European policy makers was drawn to indirect taxation. However, one of the merits of the Neumark Committee was to highlight the crucial role of direct taxation:

it must be studied – the Neumark report stated at the exordium – if, how and to what extent the abolition of Customs frontiers could also lead to the abolition of 'tax frontiers'. Another clear objective

of integration is the avoidance of all taxation and other discrimination based on nationality or tax domicile.   (IBFD 1963: 101)

Even now the Neumark report remains a finely crafted piece of
work on international taxation. The great intelligence of the report
is shown by the appreciation of European tax policy as a delicate
balance between positive and negative integration.[8] On the one
hand, tax policy at the European level should be concerned with
the abolition of subsidies to exports, distortionary tariffs, and
double taxation. This is the 'negative integration' component of
tax policy, concerned with striking down national measures that
impede the establishment of the single market. But the report
acknowledged that, once created, the market must be governed.
Hence the idea of accompanying negative integration with market-
shaping measures. The report outlined a series of far-reaching
recommendations. Among these, common principles for the definition of the tax base, a single income tax with a common structure
of scales (but not the same rates), a corporate tax based on a split-
rate system, a multi-lateral European convention against double
taxation, and, more importantly still, 'a supra-national equalisa-
tion of finances' (IBFD 1963: 101).

The Committee, in fact, was 'convinced that harmonisation of
fiscal and financial policies cannot be achieved without the adoption of compensatory measures if it is wished to avoid distortion
of competition between states'. The Committee accepted the argument that economic disparities are present even in mature federations, and consequently focused exclusively on disparities which
'carry with them effects curbing or distorting competition' (IBFD
1963: 102). In a sense, the Committee had anticipated a key issue
in the debate on the single market, monetary policy and economic
disparities, that is, the compensatory role of the EU budget in an
integrated economy.[9] Some of the policy instruments chosen by
the Committee are obviously out of date,[10] but the intuition of
the far-reaching implications of tax policy coordination is still
extremely valid.

The Committee was also well aware of the political suscepti-
bility arising from tax harmonization. Therefore it argued for

> a kind of rational compromise between the necessity of eliminating
> or at least strongly reducing, in the interest of the optimum func-
> tioning of the common market, the fiscal and financial disparities
> hindering the free play of competition between the member states

on the one hand, and the expediency of not interfering in the policy
of member states anxious to maintain national peculiarities
arising from natural conditions and/or historical evolution on the
other hand.   (IBFD 1963: 99)

Accordingly, the Committee suggested a step-by-step approach.
Tax coordination should start with turnover taxes and gradually
extend to direct taxation and the European budget. The members
of the Neumark Committee went out of their way to persuade the
six governments of the European Economic Community that
'the purpose of the Committee is not to rough out a sort of ideal
taxation system ... because the objective of the common market
is not uniformity but solely harmonisation of the tax systems'
(IBFD 1963: 100). With hindsight, however, some of the recommendations on the personal income tax and on corporate taxation
seem to have been informed by the mirage of the 'ideal tax system'.

Be that as it may, the Neumark report set the scene for the tax
initiatives of the Commission. The Commission, before launching
specific proposals, set up working parties for the discussion of
how taxation affected the competitive position of business (Farmer
and Lyal 1994: 19). It soon became clear that tax coordination
had to solve two very different problems. On the one hand, tax
havens and tax avoidance had already caused worries amongst
European tax authorities, and the working parties analyzed the
phenomenon of revenue losses caused by damaging tax competition. On the other, the common market teemed with tax obstacles
to cross-border mergers, withholding taxes on profits distributed
abroad and domestic taxes on transactions between parents and
subsidiaries of multinational corporations. In a word, international
double taxation. The situation was paradoxical in that tax coordination had to face the apparently mutually inconsistent challenges of
lack of taxation and double taxation.

Another serious issue was the free movement of capital. This
issue was investigated in 1966 by a group of experts chaired by
Professor Claudio Segre'. A chapter of the report was dedicated
to the role of European tax measures in the establishment of a
single capital market. The Segre' Committee used tax neutrality
as a yardstick for assessing tax measures. In a single capital market – this was the argument – taxes should not influence the choice
of where to invest, how to invest (directly or by means of an
intermediary), and how to finance the investment. Following the

publication of the Segre' Report (Commission 1966) the Commission submitted to the Council a comprehensive tax package (1967, Bulletin Supplement, no. 8). It is important to observe that in 1967 the first two directives on value added tax were agreed by the Council. As for direct taxation, the Commission demanded approximation of tax rates, harmonization of the tax base, and collaboration in tax collection amongst revenue authorities. A key objective of the tax package was the elimination of double taxation, with particular emphasis on the tax treatment of parents and subsidiaries and taxes on international mergers and acquisitions. On these two issues in 1969 the Commission went so far as to propose adoption of two directives, later agreed upon by the Council in 1990, that is, after twenty-one years.

In 1970 Professor van den Tempel analyzed the different systems for the taxation of profits: the classical system, the imputation and the split rate. In his independent study prepared for the Commission, van den Tempel, even though aware of the political difficulties of direct tax harmonization, did not resist the temptation to specify a final fiscal system for the Community as a whole. This time the classical system had to be selected, owing to its simplicity. In the same year, the Commission presented a proposal for a European Company Statute (OJ 1970, C124/1) which contained *inter alia* provisions on fiscal residence and its transfer from one country to another. This proposal has been revised and resubmitted a number of times (for example in 1975 and 1989) but without success. The lack of a comprehensive framework disciplining the European company as a single entity is still considered one of the major hindrances to the development of EU multinationals.

As shown in the previous chapter, 1970 was the year of the Werner Report on the achievement of monetary union. The Commission cultivated the expectation of getting concrete results on tax policy by exploiting the drive of the single currency. With the Council resolution of 22 March 1971 on 'the attainment by stages of economic and monetary union' the path to the single currency appeared settled. The resolution made explicit reference to direct taxation, demanding harmonization of taxes on interest and dividends and harmonization of corporate taxation. Another Council resolution (21 March 1972) provided ammunition in that it established that proposals for fiscal harmonization would be given priority. Once placed on the agenda – the resolution stated – proposals from the Commission would receive a Council's ruling within six months. The Commission presented proposals for company taxation in 1975. As the dynamism of the Council on economic and monetary union was short-lived (see Chapter Four), by 1975 the promise to take action on direct tax policy was long forgotten.

Three hallmarks of the early European tax policy process can already be seen. One is the preference for committees of experts and independent studies. Given the political importance of direct taxation and the inherent complexity, the Commission strategy in the 1960s and the 1970s was one of removing taxation from the political limelight. Committees of experts have the advantage of operating as fora of discussion, not as arenas of power. Most crucially, they have the advantage of providing technocratic legitimacy to the Commission. As shown in Chapter Three, the Commission is very active in 'forum politics', a type of politics conducive to learning dynamics and problem-solving attitudes.

Secondly, European direct tax policy was always combined with a macro-objective of great relevance. At the onset direct tax policy was linked to the goal of a customs union, with the Segre' Report the realization of the capital market was supposed to drive tax coordination, and in the early 1970s tax policy was 'framed' in the context of a monetary union as envisaged by the Werner Report. Hence the second hallmark of the tax strategy was the search for a drive. Be it the single currency or the European capital market, in all cases the political difficulties of harmonizing taxes were to be anaesthetized – at least according to the plans of the Commission – by inserting tax harmonization into broader and extremely desirable goals. This is yet another indication of the scarce political support for tax harmonization per se.

Third, and in blatant contradiction with the search for technocratic legitimacy, smooth policy making and anaesthetic drives, the proposals of the Commission leant towards the choice of a final or 'ideal' fiscal system. The preferences of the Commission (on the taxation of profits, the necessity to harmonize rates, and the single income tax) vary throughout the years, but the bias toward a European tax system, as opposed to limited intervention, is evident. For example, in 1975 the Commission proposed a uniform system for the taxation of profits (this time the imputation system was selected) and a compulsory range of corporate tax rates (between 45 per cent and 55 per cent). This draft directive[11] remained up until 1990 the official proposal of the Commission, but the Council was adamant in rejecting what was perceived as unduly centralization. In conclusion, the three components of the strategy of the Commission were mutually inconsistent. Technocratic legitimacy went hand in hand with the effort to nest tax proposals inside broad, shared objectives, but collided with the excessive ambition of the proposals. The bias for centralization has a negative implication. Even incremental proposals (the 1969 draft directives, for instance) were damaged by this image of centralization surrounding the proposals of the Commission. At the Council level there was strong opposition to the idea of granting the Commission even the mere general entitlement to regulate direct corporate taxation. Every specific tax concession would have been interpreted by member states as the beginning of a centralization process.

The technocratic stage

Up until the 1980s, the results achieved in tax coordination were poor. Perhaps the most important result in direct taxation was a directive on collaboration among tax authorities agreed in 1977 (no. 99/77/EEC), and even in this case the implementation of the directive was far from being satisfactory (Picciotto 1992). Learning from this disappointing record, the Commission changed its strategy when a new Commissioner, Christiane Scrivener, took the portfolio for tax policy in 1989. The aims of the new approach to tax coordination were to avoid as much as possible any political confrontation over tax centralization and national tax sovereignty, present tax proposals as a 'natural' complement to the single market design, and adhere completely to the cautious, technical, aseptic language of tax efficiency.

Let us examine these components of the technocratic strategy of the Commission step by step. To begin with, a crucial aim was to defuse the political row over the intention of the Commission to 'centralize' tax policy via excessive harmonization. As a first step, Scrivener withdrew the 1975 proposals, stressed subsidiarity as a key component of the Commission's approach to European tax policy, and removed from the official communications the taboo word harmonization. Tax coordination did not require harmonization, but only solutions to problems which, upon closer examination on a case by case base, required the intervention of the EU. In addition, the Commission pressed the Council with a limited package of measures (some of them originally submitted to the Council in 1969) referring to the removal of national withholding taxes hampering the cross-border operations of multinationals.

In striking similarity with the past, the Commission sought to exploit the drive of broader goals for European integration. This time the candidate was the single market plan boosted by the signature of the Single European Act and the 1992 deadline for the completion of a free market for people, goods, capital, and services. With the Single European Act, member states committed themselves to the removal of the barriers to the single market. Direct taxation was hardly mentioned by the White Paper preparing the ground for the single market, but the political impact of the 1992 deadline on tax policy was felt in any case. By deciding to remove an impressive number of barriers, the Single European Act implicitly stressed the negative impact of tax distortions. In a market where $n - 1$ variables are harmonized via the Single European Act, the remaining variable (in our case, taxation) became increasingly important and politically visible to policy makers and corporations.

Further, during the 1980s economic integration in Europe deepened. As a consequence, tax impediments to European operations became increasingly important for corporations and employers' organizations. In the perception of the business community the advantages of a European market without fiscal barriers became increasingly relevant. Thus in this period UNICE and other employers' peak organizations supported the Commission and its proposals for a level playing tax field with intensifying conviction.

After the attempts to fend off the charge of centralization and to exploit the single market drive, the third component of the new approach was the use of arguments drawn from the debate in public economics. Experts have always been present in the arena of direct European taxation. However, in the 1980s economists began to investigate specific tax impediments and measurable fiscal distortions with more accurate instruments. In their analyses, they provided calculations of effective tax rates. An effective tax rate condenses a number of different taxes into a synthetic measure of the cost of capital. For a firm willing to invest, it is the aggregate impact of taxes on the cost of capital, and not single taxes, that makes a difference as to whether to invest or not, how to finance the investment, and where the investment is made (at home or abroad, for example).

The key word in the policy conclusions of this school of thought is tax neutrality. The debate on tax policy revolved around the concepts of capital export neutrality and capital import neutrality. When the former is achieved there is no tax incentive to locate investment in one country rather than another. The latter instead assures that in a given country there is no tax-induced competitive advantage of a domestic company over a foreign company. Capital export neutrality and capital import neutrality can thus be employed as a yardstick for assessing the efficiency of taxes affecting cross-border company activity in the single market. Indeed, the two concepts are intimately linked to the essence of the Single European Act, the thrust of which is to eradicate obstacles to the free movement of workers, capital, and goods. Similarly, capital export neutrality and capital import neutrality can be seen as an extension of this fundamental idea to cross-border tax obstacles.

It would be a gross simplification of the reality to argue that the Commission deliberately made political use of this debate within public economics. Instead there was a convergence of the policy discourse – a new 'climate of opinion', as it were – around the key ideas of the single market, subsidiarity, and tax neutrality. Simply, the new approach of the Commission chimed with the principle of tax neutrality. At the same time, economists making use of tax neutrality were close to the policy debate as they were drafting reports for the International Monetary Fund, the Organization for Economic Cooperation and Development, think tanks such as the Institute for Fiscal Studies, and of course, the Commission itself.

Thus the Commission found itself in good company with economists arguing that tax differences between member states are acceptable, as long as they do not negatively affect neutrality. Tax diversity – this is the essential thrust of the argument – is generally acceptable because it is the result of different choices about the role of the state in the economy and the welfare state in countries which remain diverse. Moreover, a certain degree of tax competition among states stimulates efficiency. However, there are domestic taxes (for example, a withholding tax on dividends paid by a subsidiary to a parent company in another state) that have distortionary effects. It is this type of taxes which has to be coordinated by European action. This argument was instrumental in persuading member states that the Commission had definitively shunned the option of centralization. Through the calculation of effective tax rates and the cost of capital, the Commission had at its disposal a list and a measure of the most distortionary taxes (Devereux and Pearson 1989).

It was then possible to link together empirical evidence, a cautious language on tax coordination, the commitment to complete the single market, and a package of limited proposals submitted to the Council. In terms of types of policy making, this approach aimed at reducing the political salience of tax coordination, increasing the role of technical arguments for European action on taxation, and persuading member states that tax coordination was nothing more than a 'natural' (hence non-disputable and non-controversial) yet essential complement to the single market plan. It was therefore at this stage that technocratic policy making reached its climax in the European direct tax policy process.

In terms of the typology introduced in Chapter Three, the degree of political salience was lowered. Uncertainty on what should be done remained high, however. It is sufficient to observe that economic models are unable to provide an answer to the question whether the most important problem in tax policy is the lack of taxation (that is, tax avoidance and tax evasion) or the presence of double taxation. This uncertainty made tax policy amenable to technocratic politics. In fact, the discourse on tax neutrality, cost of capital and effective tax rates was instrumental in providing guidance to policy makers. In sum, high uncertainty and low political salience represent the best environment for the growth of technocratic politics.

A political implication of the technocratic approach was the formation of an advocacy coalition for tax neutrality. The Commission was the pivotal actor in this coalition. Other important actors were pressure groups such as European employers' confederations and national pressure groups. For the business community, indeed, the approach of the Commission promised less taxation on multinationals and a 'level playing field' in terms of tax neutrality. European federations of tax professionals, auditors and tax lawyers provided a bridge between the business community and the world of knowledge (see Radaelli 1997: chapter six). The Institute of Chartered Accountants, the Law Society and European level professional bodies (such as the Confédération Fiscale Européenne and the Fédération des Experts Comptables Européens) intervened in favour of the Commission's proposals bringing the opinion of the tax professional 'working daily in the tax jungle' into the policy process. Finally, an embryonic epistemic community of international taxation (composed of economists) flanked the advocacy coalition with studies on the lack of tax neutrality in the single market. Thus the tax policy process exhibited an advocacy coalition accompanied by the formation of an underlying epistemic community. This epistemic community was not a key actor in the process, although it contributed to policy development by providing measures of the tax-induced distortions in the single market.

The advocacy coalition for tax neutrality was facing a competing coalition of ministers of finance and tax authorities. This alternative coalition employed the rhetoric of sovereignty at great length (Radaelli 1997: chapter six). The political symbolism of sovereignty is particularly powerful in tax policy issues. But member states had very few technical arguments for objecting to the tax proposals of the Commission, especially because these proposals were presented as a natural complement to the decision (supported by all member states) to create a single market.

Thus the technocratic approach produced results in the short term. The Commission insisted on a limited number of corporate tax proposals amenable to close examination in technical working parties. Given the limitations and the convincing technical arguments surrounding the Commission's proposals at this stage, it was hard to argue that the Commission was demanding tax centralization. The Commission, instead, went out of its way to argue that it had abandoned the political determination to create the 'ideal' or 'final' European tax system. Member states were eventually persuaded: in 1990 the following three corporate tax measures were agreed upon by the Council:

- a directive on the common system of taxation applicable to mergers, divisions, transfers of assets and exchanges of shares between companies of different member states (the so-called mergers directive, 90/434/EEC);
- a directive against the double taxation of profits distributed between parent companies and subsidiaries of different member states (the so-called parent-subsidiary directive 90/435/EEC);
- a convention aiming for the elimination of double taxation in connection with the adjustment of profits of associated enterprises (also known as arbitration convention on transfer pricing 90/436/EEC).

The 1990 tax measures are targeted towards the aim of tax neutrality. In fact, the two 1990 directives aim at removing a series of tax obstacles to the operation of the single market. The parent-subsidiary directive covers a tax regime which had previously been regulated by a messy jungle of norms: 57 different bilateral tax treaties between 12 states, with the lack of 9 bilateral treaties between 7 member states. The mergers directive has potential because it disposes of some tax obstacles to the creation of competitive European companies. However, the implementation stage of the mergers directive has shown problems as some operations considered by the directive are not specifically provided for under national laws.

The convention protects companies who confront tax authorities of different member states in relation to transfer pricing issues.[12] By means of an appropriate arbitration procedure, the convention assures that the opinion of the company assessed by tax authorities of different member states is given due weight. The arbitration panel is compelled to reach a decision. The point is noteworthy because according to standard procedure (that is, in the absence of the arbitration convention) revenue authorities can start discussion on transfer pricing without the need to agree on a final decision. In these circumstances, lack of decision can yield double taxation because a company is requested to pay more taxes on international transfer pricing operations by country A, and country B does not adjust the tax liability accordingly. The problem with the implementation of the convention is that member states have not shown political will to use the convention, although all of them had ratified it by early 1996. The Commission and the European Court of Justice cannot intervene in this matter because conventions are excluded from the domain of the Commission and from the jurisprudence of the Court.

In short, the three tax measures examined so far represent a step in the direction of a level playing field in European taxation. More importantly still, with the 1990 decision the Council agreed to the creation of an embryonic direct corporate tax regime (two directives) managed by the Commission (and the European Court of Justice, with the important exception of the convention of transfer pricing). However, this regime is nothing more than a first step in the direction of tax neutrality. The establishment of a level playing field, presumably, also requires the adoption of directives on company law (the long-awaited European company statute) and on the taxation of savings (for example, a common European withholding tax on cross-border exchange of information) which have not as yet materialized. Looking at corporate taxes, the efficiency of the single market is still jeopardized by distortionary domestic taxes on transnational operations. Hence the Commission sought to persuade the Council to complete the 1990 package with other tax measures against double taxation (Easson 1993; Radaelli 1997). In order to maintain momentum on corporate tax policy, the Commission promoted a Committee of independent experts (the Ruding Committee, set up in 1991), with the mandate to formulate a strategy for the long term.

The mandate to the Committee, chaired by Onno Ruding, consisted of the following three questions:

> Do differences in taxation among member states cause major distortions in the internal market, particularly with respect to investment decisions and competition? In so far as such distortions arise, are they likely to be eliminated simply through the interplay of market forces and tax competition between member states, or is action at the Community level required? What specific measures are required at the Community level to remove or mitigate these distortions?
>
> (Commission 1992: 11)

As can be seen, the mandate was fully consistent with the emphasis on tax neutrality and the efficiency of the single market typical of this technocratic stage. Tax competition appeared in the mandate, mostly as a possible solution to the tax distortions in the internal market. The Commission demanded specific recommendations, that is, proposals to be dealt with on a technical basis, possibly at the lowest levels of politicization. In addressing its answers, the final Report of the Committee (Commission 1992) presented both an accurate analysis of European tax distortions, and a survey of European companies. The Ruding Committee had no hesitation in asserting that the single market was still teeming with discriminatory and distortionary taxes impeding cross-border business investment and shareholding, notwithstanding the presence of the 1990 directives. At the same time, the Ruding Report argued that the corporate tax systems of the member states had converged to a certain extent. However, the Committee hastened to add 'a large part of this convergence appears to stem from a general reduction and convergence in interest rates and inflation rates over the period. Further, much of the remainder of the reduction can be traced to just two reforms, in Germany and the UK' (Commission 1992: 166).

The Committee was unable to answer the question whether convergence was the product of tax competition or the result of 'a surge of interest in corporate tax reform' (Commission 1992: 167). On the one hand, following the drive provided by Germany and the UK, most member states had renounced to high statutory rates. At the same time, this reduction was accompanied by the broadening of the tax base. This tendency – the Committee observed – was consistent with the goal of tax neutrality. On the other, some countries pursued the aim of encouraging inward foreign investment at the expense of the goal of tax neutrality by creating special tax regimes (Commission 1992: 166–7). This was evidence of harmful tax competition because special tax regimes distort the allocation of capital. The latter does not flow where the return on investment is higher, but where taxes are lower.

As a consequence, tax competition had to be considered as a very ineffective solution to the problems of the European tax system. Not only did the Committee point out examples of damaging tax competition, it also rejected the argument that tax competition is good because it prevents an expansion of the public sector budget beyond economically efficient levels. 'If governments do indeed strive to maximise their revenues' – the Committee argued – 'international tax competition might well induce them to shift the tax burden from mobile capital on to internationally immobile factors, rather than reducing the overall level of taxation. It is also possible that tax competition might induce short-sighted governments to shift part of the tax burden on to future generations by accepting higher current budget deficits' (Commission 1992: 151).

To sum up then, the Committee found evidence of limited convergence, with the qualification that convergence had not been enough to dispose of the tax obstacles to the single market. Tax competition had little potential for solving the problem of tax-induced distortions. Quite the opposite indeed, the Committee observed that special tax regimes designed to attract internationally mobile business were an element of inefficiency in the allocation of capital. However – this is the crucial point – the Committee did not place the argument of damaging tax competition at the core of European tax policy. The members of the Committee remained convinced that the core of EU corporate tax policy should be the fight against specific tax distortions. Indeed the Report concluded that 'judging from past experience, the Committee found no convincing evidence that independent action by national governments is likely to provoke unbridled tax competition among member states and lead to a drastic and undesirable erosion of corporate tax revenues' (Commission 1992: 200). Special tax regimes were acknowledged as an element of inefficiency, however, and for this reason the Committee proposed a minimum statutory corporate tax rate throughout the Community. Apart from this, the Committee supported wholeheartedly the idea of the Commission tackling tax impediments to the single market one by one, with *ad hoc* proposals aiming at striking down discriminatory and distortionary taxes.

From technocracy to the politics of tax competition

Notwithstanding the presence of specific proposals and the work done by the Ruding Committee, the piecemeal and technocratic approach of the Commission did not produce further results after the measures agreed in 1990. Even very specific directives proposed by the Commission with the support of European multinationals were not approved by the Council. As years went by, direct tax policy in the EU became an issue with very low political salience. Partly, this result was deliberately sought by the Commission, who was striving for a non-political approach to tax coordination. However, without political determination to make concessions (in terms of abolishing domestic taxes with distortionary effects), technocratic policy making degenerated into a general neglect of direct tax coordination. Ironically, the Commission became the victim of its own success. The degree of politicization of the debate diminished, but so did the political resoluteness to coordinate taxation. A period of scarce interaction between the Commission and the Council, and a general lack of political attention, ensued. When Professor Mario Monti took the tax portfolio in 1995, there were 18 tax proposals[13] at the Council's table, but a higher number of proposals (30) had been withdrawn.

In his attempt to regain momentum for EU taxation, the new Commissioner deliberately placed tax issues within a broader political framework. The starting point was a paper presented to the informal ECOFIN (the Council of Economic and Finance Ministers) meeting of Verona during the Italian Presidency of the EU (13 April 1996). The Verona paper[14] argues that 'in the past too often discussions were confined to taxation proposals seen in isolation, thus limiting proper consideration of wider tax issues and of the framing of taxation policy within the wider context of EU policies'.

The Verona paper introduces an important innovation in the strategy adopted by the Commission for interpreting tax policy and making proposals. Instead of making a case for efficiency and tax neutrality, since Verona the Commission has insisted on the political argument that tax competition is eroding the tax base and is placing an unfair tax burden on labour. Instead of introducing proposals to be considered individually and accepted or rejected depending on their own technical validity, the Commission has advocated for a comprehensive approach. The change in strategy could not have been bigger. Moreover, tax competition, which in 1992 was perceived by the Ruding Committee as an important but not decisive feature of tax policy in Europe, has now become the corner-stone of the Commission's initiative.

Why should tax competition be at the centre of the EU tax policy? New conclusive studies on tax competition have not as yet appeared, and consequently the hypothesis of innovations in knowledge and research guiding the choice of the Commission should be rejected. The Commission itself has not produced further major research reports following the completion of the Ruding Committee Report in 1992. The strength of tax competition as a key argument lies elsewhere, and precisely in its political message.

As already hinted, the case against damaging tax competition can be made by observing that with the liberalization of capital flows and the gradual achievements of the single market, companies and investors are free to allocate capital in special tax regimes or wherever the tax treatment of investments and savings is more favourable. The existence of non location-specific activities has made central services of companies, head offices, offshore banking and insurance companies free to go where the taxes are lower. Even skilled labour can be attracted abroad – although only to a certain extent – by means of special tax incentives (Tanzi 1995).

A consequence is that countries unwilling to play the game of special tax regimes and tax incentives will be penalized in terms of significant erosion of the tax base. More importantly still, these countries would have either to tax labour more heavily, or reduce the size of their welfare state dramatically. The former option is incompatible with the objective of encouraging employment in

Europe and with the goal of fairness in the tax system. The latter is not acceptable to European governments who have already cut public expenditure in order to comply with the criteria for participation to the single currency (see the previous chapter). If capital income taxes spiral down to zero, corporations move profits to special tax regimes, and governments decide not to tax labour more heavily, there will be no resources left for funding the programmes of the welfare state.

The political message, then, is that tax coordination is a fundamental bulwark of EU public policy. Without it, the edifice of the single market, the welfare state and employment policy will soon cave in. The political attention for tax coordination – this is an explicit impact sought by the discourse on harmful tax competition – must be raised to maximum levels.

The emphasis on harmful tax competition has also an important political property. It talks directly to member states by magnifying the economic and political gains available to governments through European cooperation. By contrast, the technocratic discourse of efficiency and tax neutrality adopted by the Commission in the past – based on the selective elimination of domestic taxes hampering the growth of genuine multinational companies in Europe – highlighted gains to be reaped by companies and costs to be borne by states. In a sense, one element of success of the tax competition strategy is its appeal in terms of member states' priorities. It should be observed that, at least in the long term, both tax neutrality and the new strategy of tax competition are ways of securing collective gains. But in the short term the immediate impact of the tax competition strategy is the closure of tax havens and special tax concessions (a gain for member states in terms of revenue stabilization, but a loss for companies benefiting from special tax rules). By contrast, the immediate impact of the technocratic strategy of the early 1990s is a gain for companies and a cost for revenue authorities, compelled to give up withholding taxes (see Figure 5.1). Webb makes a similar point when he observes that the activity of the EU in corporate taxation up to the early 1990s was 'overwhelmingly oriented towards eliminating double taxation, not to increasing the ability of governments to raise revenues from corporate taxation' (Webb 1996: 24).

Further, tax competition rings a political bell in countries who, independently from their willingness, are simply unable to play the game of tax competition because the presence of domestic veto

Gains of tax coordination

Costs of tax coordination	Gains for countries	Gains for companies
Costs borne by countries		Technocratic approach (1989–94)
Costs borne by companies	Politicization – Harmful tax competition (1995–99)	

Figure 5.1 *Short-term costs and gains of different approaches to EU direct tax policy coordination*

players obstructs tax reforms at the national level (Hallerberg and Basinger 1998). The case of Germany in the 1990s, where Chancellor Kohl was unable to respond with effective domestic tax reform to the challenge of tax competition, epitomizes the appeal of EU solutions when domestic policy change is impeded by veto players.

Another political consequence of the emphasis on tax competition is that by looking at taxation *comprehensively* compromise among member states across different tax issues can be made easier. Countries such as Ireland may be unwilling to renounce to special tax regimes for corporations, but they may do so if Luxembourg agrees to a less aggressive tax policy targeted toward portfolio income and Italy freezes tax concessions camouflaged under state aid to less developed regions. The idea is to transform a series of individual zero-sum games into a larger positive sum game. By considering tax policy comprehensively, countries losing on one specific tax policy issue could have been compensated by gains in other issues. In order to facilitate this type of compromise, in the aftermath of the Verona paper, the Commission suggested member states give birth to a tax policy group composed of personal representatives of EU ministers of finance. Since the beginning, this has been a high level political group and not just one of the many technical working groups active within the Commission.

The mandate of the tax group was precisely to take a comprehensive view of tax policy in the EU. At this point the past strategy of case-by-case approach was shunned definitively and the policy discourse was redirected towards comprehensive (as opposed to piecemeal) tax policy. In its final report (October 1996[15]), the tax policy group recommended further work on the definition of unfair tax competition and on possible initiatives, 'whether legislative or not'. With the report, the Commission secured a result in terms of political commitment to go ahead with proposals.

Having achieved momentum, action has to emerge from strong political determination. The tax policy group was reshuffled. Some of the high profile members of the previous group were simply re-confirmed, and the representatives with lower political status were substituted by members with more political weight. Eventually, during the Luxembourg presidency of the EU a final deal was clinched by the ECOFIN Council on 1 December 1997. The agreement includes four elements.[16] The first is a voluntary code of conduct in business taxation. Over the period of five years, the code of conduct should provide initially a standstill on special tax regimes, and later a rollback of tax measures. The code defines what damaging tax measures are without blacklisting any particular tax regime. It is interesting to observe that the code does not use the expression *unfair* tax competition, although this term had been aired in the first meetings of the tax policy group. Instead, emphasis has been placed on what produces *damage*, thus avoiding the more sensitive question of whether certain tax decisions are fair or unfair.[17]

Turning to capital income taxation, the second component of the deal is the commitment to ensure a minimum of effective taxation of savings within the Community. The Council requested the Commission to come up with a proposal for a directive.[18] The third element is the decision to take a closer look at state aid policy, and accordingly the Commissioner for competition Karel van Miert is requested to draft clear guidelines on tax-based state aid. Special tax regimes have too often been developed under the rubric of legitimate state aid policy, thus circumventing the scrutiny of the tax Directorates of the Commission (DG XV and DG XXI[19]). Finally, the fourth element of the ECOFIN deal is the decision to resume proposals for a corporate tax directive on interest and royalty payments across borders. The Commission had already put forward proposals for a directive on this issue, but the lack of political commitment and technical problems (see Radaelli 1997: 124) had led Commissioner Scrivener to withdraw the proposed directive in 1994. Therefore the Commission prepared a new proposal for a Council directive on the taxation of interest and royalty payments made between associated companies of different member states.[20]

The EU direct tax policy process has thus changed. The picture of an advocacy coalition for tax neutrality facing ministers of finance and tax authorities has been substantially altered. So much so that the Commission itself has sought to enfeeble the boundaries between the two opposing coalitions. Indeed, the Commission has tried to steer the direct tax policy process towards a different structure, based on a decreasing importance of advocacy coalitions and on more integration amongst actors. It is as if the Commission intended to break down the walls between one coalition and another. The crucial element in this strategy has been the emphasis on tax competition. Companies have been perplexed by the decision to fight against tax competition but have not deterred from supporting the Commission because the integrated approach to EU tax policy includes also proposals against the double taxation of multinationals.[21]

However, the most important change is the increased political salience of EU direct tax policy. Technocratic politics has now become far less important than it was a few years ago. Objective uncertainty about what should be done remains objectively high, but it has been systematically reduced (at least in the subjective perceptions of policy makers) by the discourse on harmful tax competition and the ensuing threats for the single market, the welfare state and unemployment in Europe. These threats have been perceived as sufficient reasons for political leaders to act. Tax competition and its threats, therefore, have stabilized the assumptions needed for political action. In terms of the typology introduced in Chapter Three, technocratic politics has lost importance and the major shift is in the direction of political decision making.

Policy diffusion and technocratic legitimacy

The previous sections have tracked the evolution of the EU direct tax policy process. In this section I switch from process tracking to a comparison between monetary policy and tax policy, with the aim of shedding light on the mechanisms of technocratic legitimacy[22] and their limits. The colossal scope for monetary policy diffusion dwarfs the very limited results achieved in EU direct tax policy in 1990. The 1990 directives do not contain elements of convergence that could be compared to the ones achieved in monetary policy under the Treaty on the European Union. For example, no compulsory range of tax rates (or any other element that could barely suggest the drive towards a single European tax system) appears in the corporate tax directives, although the Commission had recommended it in the 1970s and the 1980s. Rather, the 1990 tax directives dispose of cross-border withholding taxes that distort business in the single market. The paradigm of tax neutrality was until recently the rationale around which EU tax policy was built. In addition, the Commission has shifted emphasis from tax neutrality to harmful tax competition, and therefore it is too early to argue that a certain shared paradigm has become *the* yardstick for policy makers.[23] The difference with monetary policy, in which both a paradigm *and* institutions were transferred, is striking.

How can one explain the limited progress in tax policy? Is member states' reluctance originated by political and cultural concerns, or, alternatively, by the lack of strong economic rationales? The cultural and political dimensions of direct taxation (suffice it to mention the link between taxation and representation, or the historical role of taxation in the formation of nation-states) have been powerful brakes. However, a similar constraint exists for monetary policy in that national currencies are both bastions of national sovereignty and elements of identification with a community of citizens. Briefly, culture and symbols of statehood are as important in tax policy as they are in monetary policy. Political considerations should favour rather than hamper tax policy coordination. In fact unbridled tax competition can destroy the welfare state (Sinn 1990): as averred, in an extreme scenario, capital is not taxed, highly skilled labour emigrates to favourable tax regimes, and revenue has to be extracted from the least well-off. This system would be unfair and would not provide enough income to support the welfare state.

As far as economic rationales are considered, if the case for the single currency draws upon the anti-inflationary paradigm of policy credibility, there is also a strong economic rationale for eliminating tax distortions in the single market (Devereux and Pearson 1989) and for limiting the welfare losses triggered by harmful tax competition (Commission 1996). Additionally, there is an economic rationale for arguing that tax coordination becomes indispensable if policy coordination is accepted in monetary policy. Indeed, the theory of second-best states that removing monetary barriers in a market in which other barriers are still present (cross-border withholding taxes are a case in point) can decrease the degree of economic welfare (Frenkel, Razin and Sadka 1991). Therefore EMU should be implemented only in conjunction with the removal of tax distortions; otherwise the efficiency of the single market would be put in jeopardy.

To sum up, the technocratic legitimacy of EU tax policy is poor in direct taxation, but *not* (or, more accurately, not only) because political, cultural and economic arguments against tax coordination are overwhelming. Accordingly, there must be something else that explains the fundamental difference between monetary and tax policy. The previous analysis of technocratic legitimacy in terms of the mechanisms of policy diffusion illuminates this difference. It has already been shown that the Treaty on the European Union has transferred elements of the German model to the whole of the EU. The EMU policy process has not created solutions for policy transfer from scratch, but has found in the German model of monetary policy and in the structural power of the Deutschmark a crucial anchor. Mimetism has been an important factor (in conjunction with the political dynamics illustrated in Chapter Four) in the diffusion of the German model through EMU.

Nothing similar has happened in the direct tax policy process. There is no anchor as far as domestic tax institutions are concerned. No one has as yet argued that the policy credibility of, say, the German tax model is greater than that of the UK institutions for tax policy. The very idea of a national tax system that could be considered optimal (or most desirable) for tax harmonization does not exist (Tanzi and Bovenberg 1990). Mimetism (and the technocratic legitimacy that it yields) cannot work in tax policy.

In this situation, it could be argued that the only realistic way of tackling tax policy in the EU is to harmonize around the average of existing systems. This is precisely what the Commission had suggested in its 1975 proposed directive, later withdrawn. But the case for harmonizing around existing tax systems is weak and ultimately flawed. Indeed, as all national tax systems are more or less sub-optimal, picking up the average of existing tax systems as the value around which tax harmonization should proceed can produce undesirable results. Indeed, the average of non-optimal national solutions is itself sub-optimal and can decrease the overall efficiency of EU taxation. Not surprisingly then, the 1975 proposed directive did not make much progress in the EU policy process and was eventually withdrawn by the Commission.

A possible, but ultimately not convincing, solution to the tax *impasse* could be articulated as follows. If national tax systems do not provide anchors, perhaps solutions elaborated through the rigorous application of optimality criteria could be more acceptable to member states. Economists have proposed not one, but a whole menu of optimal taxes. The names of many economists (for example, Kaldor, Meade, Lodin and Bradford) are associated with specific proposals for optimal structures of corporation tax. Finally, a number of British experts have prepared a proposal for a neutral corporation tax which, according to its proponents (IFS 1994), is particularly suitable for EU tax coordination.

All the same, the optimal taxation approach, although procedurally impeccable, has not produced results: optimal taxes are not on the agenda of the EU direct tax policy process. The problem is that this technocratic approach crashes against the wall of legitimacy. EU institutions have limited legitimacy in the EU policy process. They are not *Demiurges* imposing optimal models (concocted in Brussels or in ivory towers) upon different national tax institutions crafted by history and politics.[24] To paraphrase Aaron Wildavsky (1987) intellectual cogitation (in this case, the elaboration of optimal solutions external to the policy process) is never a substitute for social interaction.

To conclude, technocratic legitimacy is severely constrained in the absence of national models to be imitated. Given the limited legitimacy of EU institutions in imposing models upon member states, the most typical role of the Commission is to catalyse processes of diffusion already present in national states and considered optimal or most desirable, as typified by the case of EMU. Tax policy seems to corroborate this hypothesis. The discussion of media policy will add a qualification, however. In fact, it will be shown that the Commission is capable (to a certain extent) of devising models to be adopted by member states and later diffused throughout the Community. But at this stage, looking at the two cases of EMU and taxation alone, the main conclusion to be drawn is about the frailty of technocratic legitimacy.

Conclusions

Politicization is a rather recent characteristic of EU tax policy. Technocratic policy making represented an important stage of the EU direct tax policy process, and at the end of the 1980s the Commission sought to direct the discussion of its proposals towards technical considerations, fragmented negotiations and ultimately low political salience. A constant characteristic of the Commission's various tax strategies is the search for a 'drive'. In the 1960s the 'drives' were the customs union and the capital market, in 1970 the process of monetary union, in 1990 the Single European Act and the 1992 deadline for the completion of the single market. Tax coordination was presented as a 'natural' (non-questionable and non-controversial) complement to the different drives, in an attempt to mute the political features of tax coordination.

Results (albeit limited) were achieved thanks to this technocratic approach, but after 1990 momentum on tax coordination was lost. Nor did the mobilization of experts – a typical technocratic gambit to force stalemate – yield progress in EU corporate tax policy.[25] The mechanisms of technocratic legitimacy (mimetism in particular) did not help much. Faced with poor results and a general lack of interest, on the part of member states, to coordinate tax policy, the Commission launched a more political approach to EU taxation based on combating tax competition. It was the very EU body that is supposed to epitomize technocracy, that is, the Commission, to reject the technocratic approach.

The new political approach has the aim of putting tax policy at the core of EU policy. Whereas in the past taxation had been a policy in search of its 'drive', in more recent years tax coordination has been presented as the indispensable 'drive' to employment policy and the rescue of the welfare state. For example, the need for 'a coherent overall tax policy at the Community level' is mentioned in the strategic document on *The impact and effectiveness of the single market*.[26] The *Action plan for the single market*[27] stresses the removal of tax distortions as a key strategic target for improving the performance of the single market. At the Amsterdam European Council (16 and 17 June 1997) a resolution on growth and employment was agreed. Employment policy was linked explicitly to tax policy, not only by requesting more 'employment friendly' tax and social protection systems, but also by adding that 'the European Council has agreed concrete action on making maximum progress with the final completion of the internal market: making the rules more effective, dealing with the key remaining market distortions, and avoiding harmful tax competition'.[28]

In short, taxation is firmly on the agenda of EU policy and is no longer confined to the periphery of EU initiatives. More importantly still, with the code of conduct the EU initiative has regained the dimension of positive integration (market-shaping policy) which was stressed in 1962 by the Neumark Report. Not only does current EU tax policy aim at negative integration (eliminating distortions to the free-market), but, thanks to the code of conduct, it has also acquired a dimension of positive integration (that is, correcting the market forces and intervening on the undesirable mechanisms of competition).

This does not mean that a political approach to taxation is panacea. The politicization of the tax policy process secured agreement at the ECOFIN meeting of 1 December 1997, but effective implementation of the code of conduct and agreement on a minimum EU withholding tax on savings represent serious hurdles.[29] Be that as it may, the evolution of tax policy over the years exemplifies both the strength and the limitations of technocracy in the EU. Technocracy had an important place in this complex policy area, and during a certain phase it was the preferred strategy of the Commission. However, for tax coordination to go beyond minimal levels (that is, the three 1990 tax measures) political choice is unavoidable. EU public policy has to survive, perhaps eventually thrive, in a politicized environment, or fade into oblivion.

Notes

1 It is important to stress that tax competition can also yield positive results for citizens and companies, for example by limiting the expansion of the public sector beyond economically efficient levels. Tax competition among jurisdictions – provided that citizens can vote with their feet – ensures efficiency in the provision of public services. See Tiebout (1956) and McLure (1986).

2 Highly skilled labour is considered a relatively mobile factor. It can be hypothesized that in the future highly skilled workers will become sensitive – *coeteris paribus* – to generous tax treatment. See Zee (1996).

3 In doing so, I draw upon Easson (1993), Farmer and Lyal (1994), IBFD (1963), Radaelli (1997), official documentation published by European institutions and original research conducted for this chapter.

4 Article 100 is a general, catch-all provision. It provides that 'the Council shall, acting unanimously on a proposal from the Commission, issue directives for the approximation of such provisions laid down by law, regulation or administrative action in member states as directly affect the establishment or functioning of the common market'.

5 Article 100A provides for adoption by a qualified majority of single market measures, but fiscal measures are excluded explicitly.

6 During the intergovernmental conference leading to the Treaty of Amsterdam, the Italian delegation proposed qualified majority voting for taxation, but the proposal was rejected.

7 It should be observed that differential treatment of citizens of other countries is discriminatory only if these citizens are, in all material respects, in the same positions as a member state's own national.

8 See Scharpf (1996) on negative and positive integration.

9 This is the issue of fiscal federalism at the European level, which was debated at length in the MacDougall Report of 1977. See Commission (1977).

10 Not many people would stick to the recommendation of a common income tax, and very few would agree, thinking of corporate taxes, to the split rates of 50 per cent on undistributed profits and 15–25 per cent on distributed profits.

11 Proposal for a council directive concerning the harmonization of systems of company taxation and of withholding taxes on dividends, OJ 1975, C253/2; withdrawn by the Commission on 10 April 1990.

12 The essence of transfer pricing tax rules is to establish how transactions within a multinational (the price that a subsidiary, for example, charges to the parent company for specific components of a product) should be accounted for tax purposes.

13 Inclusive of indirect taxation.

14 The title of the paper is *Taxation in the European Union*, SEC(96) 487 final, 20 March 1996.

15 European Commission, *Taxation in the European Union: report on the development of tax systems*, COM(96) 546 final, Brussels, 22 October 1997.

16 See Council conclusions on fiscal package, as published by Official Journal C 2, 6 January 1998.

17 The code of conduct is strengthened by the project undertaken by the Organisation for Economic Cooperation and Development on

harmful tax competition. Further to the OECD report on this project (approved in 1998 with the abstention of Luxembourg and Switzerland) a forum was established. The OECD forum will scrutinize preferential tax regimes and take initiatives against harmful tax competition. Although this is not the subject in this book, it is clear that the success of the EU code of conduct is linked to the future of the OECD initiatives. Tax cooperation in a limited area such as the EU runs the risk of improving the competitive position of countries outside the EU (Genschel and Plümper 1997).

18   The Commission thus submitted a proposal for a Council directive to ensure a minimum of effective taxation of savings income in the form of interest payments within the Community, COM (1998) 295, 20 May 1998. Member states can choose between the 20 per cent withholding tax and exchange of information on non-resident savings.

19   It should be noted that in June 1998 responsibility for direct taxation was shifted from DG XV to DG XXI. Thus the entire tax policy of the Commission falls under the responsibility of DG XXI.

20   The proposal was presented on 4 March 1998, COM(1998) 67 final.

21   However, the business community has expressed its perplexities on certain aspects of the new strategy of the Commission, such as the minimum withholding tax on savings. The *Wall Street Journal* has manifested scepticism on several occasions, for example on 29 July 1998 'Economists say no to tax harmonization'. See also the statement of UNICE's president Dirk Hudig in the Italian daily *Il Giornale*, 16 July 1998, 'Gli industriali UE bocciano Monti' (EU entrepreneurs fail Monti). See also UNICE (1998).

22   As defined in Chapter Three. The three mechanisms of technocratic legitimacy are coercion, mimetism, and normative pressure.

23   Further, only a limited degree of tax neutrality has been achieved. As observed by the Ruding Committee and by more recent reports of the Commission (Commission 1992; Commission 1996), the single market still contains a number of tax distortions which have not been eliminated so far.

24   See Steinmo (1993) for an analysis of tax systems in terms of historical institutionalism.

25   Interestingly, the Ruding Committee included experts from the business community and was not dominated by academic experts. The idea was to flesh out proposals with the consensus of experts who knew what tax distortions meant 'in the real world' to European businesses.

26 COM(96) 520 final, 30 October 1996, page 31.

27 Commission CSE97–1, final, 4 June 1997, see page 5 and 6.

28 See the Resolution of the European Council on Growth and Employ-
    ment, annex to the Amsterdam European Council of 16 and 17 June
    1997, Presidency Council.

29 Although exaggerated and distorted by the tabloid press, the high
    political temperature reached by Anglo-German relationships in tax
    policy (in November–December 1998) shows the unforeseen (and
    undesirable) consequences of politicization. At the climax of this
    episode, with the British popular press portraying the German finance
    minister as 'the most dangerous man in Europe', there was the risk
    of dissolving the real tax issues into a vortex of ideological political
    confrontation.

CHAPTER SIX

Media ownership policy: the limits of technocratic regulation

With the assistance of Alison J. Harcourt

Background: the media and media policy

The West-European media industry offers a paradigmatic case of dramatic change. Up until twenty years ago, this was one of the most regulated industries, being characterized by the overwhelming presence of public televisions and radio stations. The press market was purely domestic if not regional. Cross-media ownership was not an issue. The situation has now completely changed, due to market trends, the dynamics of technology, and, most crucially, media policy decisions. In order to introduce media policy and the issue of ownership regulation it is useful to outline what media policy should be according to the prevailing paradigms. This section will be mainly concerned with providing the reader with the indispensable elements for understanding this complex policy area. As such, it will not touch upon the issue of technocracy in the EU, which is instead the object of the rest of the chapter.

Characteristically, media policy has been the object of tensions originating from the collision among the market, technocracy, and democracy. In short, *laissez-faire*, 'benign technocracy' and pluralism represent three alternative paradigms or normative theories.[1] In the real world, media policy is almost invariably the resultant of the (often unstable) equilibrium among them. According to the *market paradigm*, the media industry should be governed as any other industry. In order to sell copies and to broadcast as widely as possible, the media must inform objectively and give people what they want. The market is not a jungle, however. Thus public policy performs the duty of maintaining the market as open as possible. All the same, the market paradigm assigns a very limited role to public policy. The list of public policy DONTs (for example, do not prevent the growth of the industry with unnecessary rules) is much longer than the list of DOs. The problem with this approach is that the unconstrained, deregulated media market has not produced diversity, but, at least so far, homogenization of production, standardization of content, press oligopolies and concentration of production in broadcasting.[2]

For this reason, and in contrast with what has happened in the USA, policy makers in Western Europe have emphasized the social responsibility of the media. The latter is not just any other business (McQuail 1994: chapter 6). In sharp contrast with the market paradigm, the second paradigm assumes that the press, radio and television speak to citizens, not to consumers. There is a specific and socially responsible public character of the media, as shown by the political function of the media in democratic political systems, the educational and informative roles of the media, and the negative political implications of oligopolies and monopolies of ideas and information. With the exception of Luxembourg, Western Europe has witnessed the emergence of the *social responsibility* paradigm (Humphreys 1996). In short, the media industry should be governed by public policy in such a way as to guarantee the cultural function of the media (as opposed to commercialism) and freedom of expression. However, critics of the social responsibility doctrine have observed that it was a form of benign, yet ultimately anti-democratic, technocracy. For if the development of the media industry is put in the hands of the state without any countervailing market-societal force, there is no guarantee that it will respond to the real interests of the citizens, and not to the interest of politicians and bureaucrats. Thus this paradigm has been accused of being elitist, paternalistic, bureaucratic, and essentially technocratic.

The third paradigm puts instead a premium on *pluralism*, rather than on the public control of the media. Pluralists envisage the development of non-state and non-market communication systems (from community radios to media cooperatives), substantial decentralization, an informed public debate, social diversity and respect for minorities, and perhaps new forms of free electronic democracy (Keane 1992). The problem with this paradigm is that it has been, at least so far, considered idealistic.

Having described the three normative approaches, what can be said of the evolution of media policy in the real world? To begin with, there is a fundamental difference between the press and broadcasting. The press, historically, has been recognized as a bulwark of democracy. No sincere democrat has ever made the case for state control of the press. Quite the contrary, more typically the case has been made for press freedom. This theme has accompanied the disfranchisement of the press from state censorship, the battle against the political management of the news (Keane 1991), and the issue of editorial independence. Radio and television, instead, have been the object of comprehensive, systematic and strict regulation. Historically, there were three important rationales for this. They were the technical rationale (essentially, the scarcity of frequencies, leading to a situation similar to what economists define a natural monopoly), the economic rationale (if a good is a natural monopoly, there is an economic rationale for tight public regulation), and most crucially the political rationale. The latter relates to 'the effective capacity' of the broadcast media 'to focus public attention, to contribute to the creation of public opinion, to legitimise (or de-legitimise) public policy, and even directly to influence voting behaviour' (Humphreys 1996: 114).

Thereupon, public service broadcasting systems have traditionally dominated the broadcast media (whereas the press has witnessed the proliferation of free newspapers). Their growth in Europe has followed the path of the so-called public-service model, also known as the *service public* model (Blumler 1992), which shares the key characteristics with the social-responsibility paradigm. As described by Blumler, the model is based on the following criteria: non-commercialism, cultural-educational vocation, respect for pluralism and diversity in content, ethic of comprehensiveness, and generalized mandates (this means that broadcasting systems are bound to their public service mission by acts of parliaments, or charters, licenses and concessions). Additionally, Blumler lists a final criterion, 'place in politics'. In the democracies of Western Europe, public broadcasters have been, in Blumler's language, typical creatures of the states. On the one hand, this has contributed to the quality of public discourse and has resulted in a major emphasis on news and education, instead of entertainment. But of course, 'place in politics' also yields politicization of the editorial boards, direct intervention of political parties, and, in the worst scenario, politicization runs the risk of transforming the public service into a technocratic machinery providing the 'voice of the state'.

Be that as it may, the policy paradigm of *service public* remains an important trait of European media policy. Even the Amsterdam Treaty (June 1997) guarantees it. The protocol to the Treaty states[*] that 'the system of public broadcasting in the Member States is directly related to the democratic, social and cultural needs of each society and to the need to preserve media pluralism'. All the same, the last twenty years or so have witnessed a sea change in media policy. Public service broadcasting systems are still present throughout Europe, but the old picture of public dominance has been transformed by the process of deregulation. In turn, deregulation has been buttressed by political determination of European leaders willing to unleash private forces in the media industry, a change in the market of ideas,[3] market trends, the pressure of the advertising lobby,[4] and the technological challenge. The traditional technical rationale based on the scarcity of frequencies has now become obsolete in the era of cable, satellites, digital television, and the internet.

The European Commission, with its initiatives for the deregulation of utilities, accompanied this process. Hence an incisive process of deregulation ensued. The idea was to encourage (via deregulation and a certain relaxation of media ownership rules) the emergence of new commercial broadcasting operators and the exploitation of new technologies. The impressive wave of liberalization and deregulation, roughly coinciding with the EU's 1986 Single European Act, saw the introduction of private operators in terrestrial, cable, satellite television and radio broadcasting (up until the mid-1980s, only Italy, Luxembourg and the UK had private television broadcasting). This was accompanied by the regulation of the recently privatized-liberalized market, for example via the introduction of regulatory bodies and rules on programmes. This process of liberalization and regulation is not unique to the media, but represents a major characteristic of the politics of regulation in Europe and North America throughout the 1980s (Majone 1990). In terms of the language introduced in the previous chapters, the first two steps represent an attempt to strike a balance between negative and positive integration, that is, between the elimination of obstacles to the growth of a market and rules that provide direction to the market itself. As will become clear in the remainder of the chapter, the EU is facing a similar problem of drawing the boundaries between negative and positive integration in the regulation of cross-media ownership.

Although concern has been expressed about excessive regulation of the newly liberalized media market, the fact remains that the new rules were introduced with the aim of assisting and possibly governing a process of liberalization. The main drive was towards liberalization, not towards regulation. An important issue raised by liberalization has been the concentration of the media markets. Concentration takes different forms, such as industrial concentration (that is, the reduction in the number of competitors), market dominance (and the abuse of dominant positions), and editorial concentration. As for the latter, a media market where different units (newspapers, radios, and televisions) respond to a unique holding producing the main news and the editorial line for all of them is far from pluralism (Humphreys 1996: 66–7). In addition, these forms of horizontal concentration can be accompanied by vertical concentration, a term denoting the control of different stages of production by the same company.[5]

Concentration of ownership is a real problem in broadcasting.[6] The broadcasting industry has not become similar to the press in its heyday, when different newspapers provided effective pluralism and a lively public debate. The huge costs and the risks associated with market entry into a very new market have resulted in the emergence of a few media giants. Regulating ownership at the national level has been very problematic, for a number of reasons. First, a consequence of the liberalizing drive has been that rules of media ownership and cross-media ownership have been relaxed (with the aim of assisting the growth of the newly deregulated markets). Second, and in striking similarity with the process of harmful tax competition described in Chapter Five, countries have been compelled to relax their rules: otherwise companies had gone towards more favourable regulatory regimes. If tax policy is characterized by the existence of tax havens, the media industry has seen a similar expansion of the offshore-deregulated centres. Luxembourg is both a tax centre luring the savings of Europeans who do not want to be taxed at home and a deregulated media regime attracting companies willing to broadcast throughout Europe with the lowest regulatory impediments. Third, in countries such as France, Germany and Italy the regulation of ownership has been extremely reactive, more the public acceptance of a *fait accompli* than the expression of proactive governmental behaviour. Thus some regulatory regimes have merely accepted the evolution of the market. Finally, markets have been changing so quickly that it has become increasingly problematic to provide a definition of market concentration. Concentration in a dynamic multi-media market can be overestimated easily. A company securing a dominant position in one market can still be subject to fierce competition if that particular market's boundaries are blurring with the ones of a contiguous media market.

Indeed, media companies have combined strategies of diversification with those of internationalization. Cross-national market planning and international mergers and acquisitions have transformed the structure of the media industry (Sanchez-Tabernero *et al.* 1993). The centre of gravity of market operations is no longer the national market, but the European dimension, if not, for the largest companies, the global market. In the past there were national mono-media markets, whereas the current situation is one of a single European multi-media market. Cross-media concentration, therefore, has become a very serious issue for European policy makers and for the EU. The press has pursued multi-media diversification strategies, big business and financial consortia (previously not involved in the media) have diversified in the new media, and national commercial broadcasting concerns have internationalized their market activity (Humphreys 1996: chapter 6; Sanchez-Tabernero *et al.* 1993). This has raised the issue of regulating concentration across media markets at the EU level.

New technologies have been fundamental in this process of change, especially in the broadcasting industry. Geostationary satellites, digital transmission, the convergence between internet, telecommunications and television, and fibre optic cables have led to more integrated markets. The concentration of financial capital indispensable for exploiting new technologies explains the growth of large multi-media conglomerates operating in different countries. In turn, concentration of financial capital leads to concerns about the future of cultural and political pluralism in a European market dominated by a few multi-media players. So far no directive on media ownership concentration has been formally submitted to the Council. Yet an embryonic (albeit incomplete) governance regime is slowly emerging, as detailed in the remainder of this chapter.

Exploring EU media ownership policy:
the key questions

For the reasons outlined above, the regulation of media ownership
has become a European issue. In addition, the expansion of media
companies into adjacent communications markets raises problems
of analysis and content. In terms of substantive content, the convergence of telecommunications, information technology and media
is a challenge for European institutions. At what level should media
ownership be regulated? With what instruments? And for which
objectives? As will be shown below, these questions have spawned
a debate between and within European institutions. Analytically,
convergence poses the dilemma of where to draw the boundaries
of this policy area. The object of analysis is extremely elusive.
Where does EU media policy 'begin' and 'end'? The problem is
well known to policy analysts. Policy is not an objective datum
but must be reconstructed for interpretative purposes, as illustrated by Heclo in his classic article on policy analysis. In his
own words:

> Policy does not seem to be a self-defining phenomenon; it is an
> analytic category, the contents of which are identified by the analyst
> rather than by the policy-maker or pieces of legislation or adminis-
> tration. There is no unambiguous datum constituting policy and
> waiting to be discovered in the world. A policy may usefully be
> considered as a course of action or inaction rather than specific
> decisions or actions, and such a course has to be perceived and
> identified by the analyst in question. Policy exists by interrogating
> rather than intuiting political phenomena.   (Heclo 1972: 85)

In short, there is an interpretative challenge underlining all policy
studies. Yet media ownership policy is particularly elusive and
difficult to define. The very actions of European institutions in this
area witness the shifting boundaries of the policy, as will be illustrated below. It would be a gross mistake to identify media policy
with the initiatives for new European legislation, thus ignoring
what the European Court of Justice and the Directorate General
IV competent for competition policy have achieved, even in the
absence of specific legislation for media ownership policy. A comprehensive analytic grid is therefore needed. Further, as media
ownership policy is still subject to confrontations about what this

policy should be, particular attention should be drawn to the ideational dimension of policy. What are the main beliefs, the conceptual paradigms, and the norms that the builders of EU media policy discuss?

A solution to these analytic puzzles comes from a recent comprehensive study of the single market conducted by Armstrong and Bulmer (1998). Drawing upon previous theoretical work on international regimes by American scholars, they present the concept of 'governance regimes' for the study of single market policies. The reference to governance is appropriate for the examination of policy development in a political system bereft of a formal government. Governance regimes – Armstrong and Bulmer (1998: 72) explain – 'reflect one admixture of rules, procedures and norms embedded within the systemic context. Procedurally, each governance regime comprises the prevailing admixture of institutions, rules and norms together with the relevant policy players'. They add: 'important tasks in examining any governance regime include identifying the boundaries of the governance regime, its characteristics and the participants' (Armstrong and Bulmer 1998: 72).

Following this approach, an important goal in this chapter is to explore the boundaries of the governance regime in EU media ownership policy, by drawing attention both to the *ideational* dimension and to the dimension of political *action*. Ideas and participants – I will argue – are cemented in advocacy coalitions. Adversarial coalitions differ in terms of participants and beliefs and compete on two interrelated dimensions. For one, competition revolves around the ideational boundaries of the governance regime. For another, and closely linked to the former dimension, coalitions compete for the control of the governance system.

The two dimensions need further explanation. Ideas, paradigms and beliefs are important resources because (a) they provide a common identity – an 'ideational glue', to paraphrase Sabatier (1993) – to different actors and (b) they are instrumental in placing the issue onto the EU agenda in a manner which favours a specific coalition and not another. Therefore part of the conflict is all about problem definition (Rochefort and Cobb 1994). Is media ownership policy a problem of typical single market legislation, an issue of pluralism (and, deep down, cultural policy), or simply a domain of technological convergence to be assisted by appropriate EU action?

Harmonization, pluralism and convergence identify different boundaries of the governance regime. But the clash is not restricted to
intellectual debate, and it is at this point that the second dimension
matters. Proponents of the three different approaches compete for
the control of the governance regime. In this case the conflict is
placed directly within the policy process. An interesting question
– given the aims of this book – is whether the two dimensions of
conflict (ideational and political) have structured policy development
along the lines of bureaucratic politics, technocratic politics or overt
politicization?

These considerations lead to the key questions addressed by
this chapter:

- What are the main characteristics (coalitions, beliefs, and policy
  outcomes) of the governance regime? How is the balance between negative and positive integration being struck? Do forces
  for liberalization prevail over forces for disciplining the media
  market?
- What are the major arguments used in EU media ownership
  policy? Do technical arguments (for example, arguments based
  on the need to harmonize national rules in a single market)
  clash with more political arguments (for example, arguments
  for pluralism and cultural diversity), and with what results in
  terms of policy development?
- Do the shifting boundaries of the governance regime pre-empt
  the 'pillarization' of media ownership policy and thus make
  bureaucratic politics (as defined in Chapter Three) impossible?
- If bureaucratic politics is limited, to what extent does technocracy represent a major characteristic of the EU media ownership policy process? Can media policy avoid politicization and
  if so with what implications?
- Is the Commission pushing for a technocratic solution or,
  alternatively, does politicization emerge even within the Commission itself?

The next section will flesh out an important component of the
governance regime, that is, the origins of the debate on EU legislative instruments. After a start in conformity with technocratic policy
making, the policy process has become more politicized. Two additional sections will explain how different actors interact and give
shape (through conflictual interaction, the use of competition policy
even in the absence of EU directives, and the jurisprudence of the

ECJ) to the governance regime. Finally, I will assess the govern-ance regime by considering the four-fold typology introduced in Chapter Three and discuss to what extent does EU media regulatory policy follow the paths of technocracy, bureaucratic politics or political decision making.

Building a governance regime: political debate and technocratic outcomes[7]

At the outset the European media industry was perceived by the Commission as yet another sector to be liberalized. Problems of concentration and pluralism were hardly noticed by the Commis-sion in the 1984 Green Paper on the liberalization of the broad-casting market. The very title of the Green Paper, *Television without frontiers: green paper on the establishment of the common market for broadcasting* (COM 300, 1984) was revealing. The EU – this was the argument of the Commission – had to intervene in media policy with the aim of liberalizing the market and providing the necessary rules for the development of a single market in this sector. The inefficiencies produced by national regulations ought to be removed thanks to a proposed directive on television 'with-out frontiers'. Efficiency – the Commission claimed – was the only rationale for EU action. Not surprisingly, the Green Paper was produced by Directorate General (DG) III, responsible for the development of industrial policy.

This initial move by the Commission had the clear objective of isolating the debate on media policy from wider political discus-sions of pluralism and cultural diversity. Briefly, the approach was technocratic. But the gambit backfired, at least to a certain extent. Shortly after the release of the television without frontier (TWF) Green Paper, the European Parliament produced a number of requests for media concentration legislation to accompany the liberalizing TWF directive. The European Parliament did not at all see media policy as a problem of market efficiency; rather, media concentration was viewed politically as a threat to democracy, the freedom of speech and pluralist representation. Along these lines, the EP produced three documents containing precise demands to the Commission during negotiations leading up to the 1989 TWF directive: a 1985 Resolution;[8] a 1986 official request to the Commission; and the 1987 Barzanti Report.[9] Each time it was requested that the Commission be granted the legal resources to safeguard media pluralism within the context of liberalization.

However, when the TWF directive was agreed upon by the Council in 1989 it contained no provisions for anti-concentration measures. The directive contains only one very limited technical measure that indirectly affects media concentration. This is that broadcasters must reserve ten per cent of their transmission time or, alternatively, at least ten per cent of their programming budget for European works by independent producers. Unlike at the national level, where the deregulation of the media industry was accompanied by rules covering cross-ownership, the directive contained no anti-concentration measures. In response to the calls for legislation on pluralism, the Commission claimed that liberalization of the media industry would automatically produce pluralism and diversity. For DG III, broadcasting, like any other service or good, required free access to the internal market. This belief was boosted by the timing of the TWF directive. In fact, TWF was negotiated around the time of the Single European Act, when the argument of liberalization in the interest of the single market reached its climax.

The tone of the debate on media concentration leading up to the 1989 TWF directive, however, was not technocratic. The discussion was not reduced – as DG III wished – to technical arguments concerning industrial policy within the single market. The European Parliament was able to insert in the debate the theme of pluralism.[10] As hinted above, the 1989 TWF directive establishes a legal framework for the cross-border transmission of television programmes thereby creating a single audio-visual market. A media company may only be regulated in the country of transmission, not reception. Herewith the Commission aims to strengthen the competitiveness of the national media industries thereby strengthening the European market against wider forces in the international market. The directive shows how the initiators of the governance regime were able to impress a mark of depoliticization to the TWF directive. But this was a Pyrrhic victory. A battle was won by technocrats, but not the whole war!

On the one hand, the implementation of TWF revealed its consequential effects in terms of European level mergers, acquisitions and joint ventures. This prompted further political demands for concentration control from the European Parliament. On the other, certain MEPs from the UK and Italy feared a repeat at the EU level of domestic scenarios wherein liberalization and deregulation produced concentration of the media industry in the absence of specific rules on ownership. Accordingly, the European Parliament again took issue with the Commission over media concentration. No less than two Resolutions and two working papers[11] were put out by the European Parliament between 1990 and 1992. In response, the European Commission (DG III) embarked upon the issue of media ownership and released its first Green Paper on the issue in 1992.[12] The governance regime was widened as to include media ownership.

The conflict over the boundaries of the governance regime

In the 1992 Green Paper, the Commission, as it had with TWF, defined media concentration as an issue of liberalization and consolidation of the European industry within the internal market. However, the Commission had to accept that the discussion would be open, instead of being restricted to technocratic circles. Official opinions were sought and given by the European Parliament,[13] the Economic and Social Committee,[14] member states, national interest groups, national government departments and European federations. In the Green Paper the Commission called for consultation papers from interest groups to consider three possible courses of action.[15] This wide consultation on the initiative (culminating in a public hearing, April 1993) served only to enmesh the Commission in a wider political debate. In addition, the process of consultation saw public interest groups raising their voices. Among others, federations of journalists, public service broadcasters, consumer organizations, church groups, and small companies posed the question of whether pluralism should be protected by further EU action in media policy. The Commission sent three questionnaires to interested parties and actively encouraged a wide participation to the debate. The responses to the first questionnaire were so numerous that they comprise a five-volume document! The second questionnaire spawned an even wider response.

The increase in the number of participants to the policy process is an indicator of politicization as opposed to technocratic policy making. However, another element leading to politicization was the conflict within the Commission itself over problem definition.

127

It is useful to suspend the narrative here and look at the different positions within the Commission because they are the most evident illustration of the impossibility of a smooth technocratic policy-making process even within the body which supposedly incarnates technocracy.

As mentioned above, one of the bones of contention in media policy is the ideational domain. What should media policy serve for? What should its aims be? Should it be a policy for the European industry, the single market, or the protection of cultural diversity in Europe? Once an issue has been placed onto the public agenda, conflict over the alternatives (that is, which policy responses should be given to a certain issue) arises (Kingdon 1984). The Commission, far from being a unitary actor, has been split over media ownership regulation, as illustrated by Harcourt's study (1998) of different policy frameworks within the Commission. Up until 1992, the issues of European media markets and policies for the media industry were firmly in the hands of DG III, but since the debate on media ownership has entered the agenda of the Commission a number of different DGs have competed intensively. The main DGs involved in this conflict over the boundaries of the governance regime have been DG III (industrial policy), DG XV (single market), DG X (culture), DG XIII (technology and information society) and occasionally DG I (external relations). What are their main beliefs? Succinctly, for DG III media policy is yet another case of industrial policy. The European media industry is facing the challenge of global competition. Therefore EU policy should assist the growth of European media companies by liberalizing markets and, if necessary, by accepting concentration in order to compete with non-European multi-media firms.

DG XV sees media policy as a typical single market policy. The core belief of this 'single market' approach is that national rules on cross-media ownership should be harmonized. For example, all member states should agree to a directive establishing a threshold on concentration at the European level and across different media. The aim in this approach is to provide a level playing field without great divergences between one country and another in the regulation of media ownership. A patchwork of different national regulations is the main obstacle to a single market for the media industry.

DG X, together with the European Parliament, is an outspoken partisan of pluralism. According to DG X, EU initiatives should take inspiration from Article 128 (introduced by the Treaty on the European Union signed at Maastricht) and not from single market or industrial policy considerations. Article 128 states that the Community 'shall contribute to the flowering of the cultures of the member states'. This approach was strengthened by the protocol to the Amsterdam Treaty on the 'public service', as hinted above. The protocol sets a limit to further negative integration. Namely, action against public funding of the media providing public service shall be limited. However, the protocol stresses that funding should not affect 'trading conditions and competition in the Community to an extent which would be contrary to the common interest'. Therefore, it remains to be seen whether the protocol will curb the liberalizing initiatives of the Commission or not.

By contrast, DG XIII, in its effort to create the pre-conditions for the information society, places the convergence between different technologies at the centre of its proposals. Media policy should fit with the wider picture of convergence of all communications technologies. A consequence is that the peculiarity of media policy (that is, the fact that it touches upon fundamental issues of freedom and cultural diversity) is lost. DG XIII is a staunch proponent of liberalization and suggests that 'constraints' to the growth of media companies should be relaxed and ultimately removed. Concentration is not perceived as a major danger of liberalizing policies.

Finally, DG I is concerned over the external policy implications of a possible directive on media ownership. International pressure for liberalization comes from the USA, the World Trade Organization (WTO) and the Organization for Economic Cooperation and Development (OECD). The Commission met with strong opposition by US broadcasters to the small European programming provision included in the TWF directive and the US government took the issue to General Agreement on Tariffs and Trade (GATT). When the Uruguay Round eventually ended in 1994, the EU managed to obtain an opt-out for audio-visual products. However the USA is continuing to protest against the opt-out.[16] The USA is also exerting indirect pressure on Europe with its 1996 Telecommunications Act. European media companies are demanding similar deregulation of convergence in Europe. The companies argue that they may be left behind US firms if they are not also allowed to compete in adjacent markets.

The conflict within the Commission has been exacerbated by the reshuffling of competencies for media policy. In 1992 single market initiatives were transferred from DG III to DG XV, but responsibility for media regulations remained with DG III 'under temporary status'. With the inception of the Santer Commission (1995) the portfolio for media was assigned to the Commissioner for the single market, Mario Monti.

How has the policy process evolved since 1992 (the year when media ownership entered the Commission's agenda)? On the one hand, the European Parliament has continued to press for legislation. In its 1994 Fayot/Schinzel Resolution[17] the European Parliament voted in favour of tough restrictions on European media ownership. On the other, the Commission proceeded with extreme caution, due to the increased political sensitivity of media policy and to internal conflicts. In October 1994 DG XV published a second Green Paper entitled 'Follow up to the consultation process relating to the Green Paper on pluralism and media concentration in the internal market – an assessment of the need for Community action'.[18] In this paper, drafted by DG XV, the internal market argument resurfaces. The paper argues for specific legislation based on harmonized concentration rules to be applied at the European level. A major aim in the paper is to dispose of a regulatory patchwork and establish uniform EU rules. These rules should be based on threshold of audience shares, for example a 30 per cent limit in national and regional markets across all media (TV, radio and press). Instead of measuring concentration through advertising shares, turnover or other typical market indicators, the Commission opts for audience share.

Due to the high political sensitivity of media concentration and the fact that the European Parliament had increased its powers following the 1992 Maastricht Treaty, the Commission thought it important to gain the support of the Parliament's Committee on Culture, Youth, Education and the Media, the most ardent proponent of the pluralist argument. This argument was reverberated within the Commission by DG X. It is important to bear in mind the characteristics of EU public policy making. Before a proposal is formally submitted to the Parliament and the Council, it has to be agreed by the Commission as a whole. The College of Commissioners is the body where proposals coming from one Commissioner are discussed. Therefore a Commissioner – in the case under examination, Professor Monti responsible *inter alia* for DG XV – has to muster support within the College before a draft becomes a formal proposal for a directive. Consequently, the fact that the preoccupations of the European Parliament have been constantly reverberated by DG X should not be underestimated. This explains why Commissioner Monti has been talking to the European Parliament with an eye to internal consensus in the College of Commissioners.

In 1995 the positions of the Commission and the European Parliament seemed closer than ever. On the one hand, the Parliament accepted that a proposal for media regulation should have been prepared by using the logic of the single market, that is, harmonization of the regulatory patchwork. On the other, in September 1995 Commissioner Monti gave a speech before the Cultural Committee in which he declared himself to be personally in favour of an initiative which would seek to safeguard pluralism.[19]

Having secured support from the most reluctant institution (the European Parliament), Commissioner Monti felt prepared to present a proposal for a directive on media ownership to the Commission's College. Years of consultation appeared to have secured momentum and a certain maturation of the debate. As Kingdon (1984) shows, an important element in the public acceptance of policy decisions is the 'softening-up' of solutions. Commissioner Monti therefore submitted a draft on 24 July 1996. However, on this occasion Commissioners Brittan (DG I) and Bangemann (DG XIII) found the draft too strict. The draft was reconsidered by the Chefs du Cabinet and resubmitted on 4 September 1996. But this time, somewhat unexpectedly, it was Commissioner Oreja (DG X) to express concern over the relative neglect of pluralism in the draft.

One possible reason for this lack of support is that in this period the protection of pluralist issues received a major blow in the context of the renewal of the 1989 TWF directive (ratified in 1996). The Parliament – with the support of Oreja – proposed amendments based on pluralist issues (content of programming, protection of minors against harmful programmes, advertising rules and extending the scope of the directive to new services) but they were rejected by the Council. In the eyes of the Parliament and Commissioner Oreja, the protection of pluralism had become more difficult. Accordingly, a media ownership directive which had not been explicitly targeted towards pluralism (but remained essentially a single market proposal with a few concessions to democratic considerations) was not enough. Unsurprisingly then, in October 1996 the European Parliament published the Tongue Report on pluralism and media ownership containing harsh criticisms of the Commission.

The Commission was unable to appreciate the issue-linkage between the renewal of TWF and the proposal on media concentration. More importantly, the discussion of the new TWF spawned a highly political debate on the neglect of the European Parliament in crucial questions of democracy. The European Parliament – a directly elected body – was being humiliated by the Council when it was seeking to protect the freedom of citizens and their cultural diversity. This wider concern about the EU democratic deficit spilled over the discussion of the proposal for media ownership. A proposal that originally should have been discussed on its own merits in terms of strict single market logic became enmeshed with nothing less than the debate on the democratic deficit of the EU!

Following this episode, Monti sought support within the College of the Commissioners on two other occasions, that is on 18 December 1996 and on 12 March 1997, but without success. The proposal ran the risk of falling between the two proverbial stools. Commissioners such as Brittan and Bangemann pressed for more liberalization and for an explicit linkage between media and the information society, whereas Oreja raised cultural and democratic issues. Monti went out of his way to secure consensus, and altered the proposal to make it more palatable to Bangemann. But each time the draft was presented there were new objections within the College. In March 1997 Brittan was not persuaded and, somewhat unexpectedly, Santer's cabinet was less than supportive.

In short, the Commission has been unable, at least so far, to submit a proposal for consideration to the Council and the European Parliament. But a governance regime is not limited to the presence of directives. It extends to what the Commission can do in terms of its power in competition policy (the domain of DG IV) and to the initiatives of the European Court of Justice. It is to DG IV and the European Court of Justice that we now turn briefly, with the aim of completing the analysis of the embryonic media governance regime.

Competition policy and the activity of the European Court of Justice

Under competition policy, the European Commission has direct authority to make decisions that are not subject to approval by the Council of Ministers or the European Parliament, only to review by the European Court of Justice. Within the Commission, DG IV has responsibility for competition decisions and houses the Merger Task Force. Due to the special status of media falling under cultural policy at the level of the member state, DG IV has over the years developed a special policy towards Europe's media industry.

Since the 1989 TWF directive, a significant number of cross-European media mergers have been officially decided under EU competition policy (Harcourt 1999). Many further recommendations have been made on an informal basis directly with media companies and national government decisions are often influenced by the European Commission.

DG IV firstly applies competition law to the broadcasting industry according to Articles 85, 86, and 90 as defined under the Treaty of Rome. This occurs when agreements between companies are seen to come into conflict with the creation of a single market or there is generally a perceived threat to competition through cartels, monopolies or mergers. Article 85 prohibits private sector anti-competitive agreements and Article 86 prevents the abuse of dominant position. Articles 85 and 86 are applied to the public sector by Article 90. DG IV's main concern when applying these articles is that markets remain open and identifiable entry barriers are removed.

Previous to 1990, all Commission competition decisions were made under Articles 85 and 86 of the Treaty of Rome. From 1990 onwards, merger decisions were made under the 1989 Merger Regulation,[20] although joint venture decisions continued to be made under Articles 85 and 86. The Merger Regulation required proposed mergers with global sales revenues totalling over five billion ECU to notify DG IV for permission. Notification allowed companies to receive a quick decision from the Commission (within one month). In April 1997, the Merger Regulation was amended to include joint venture decisions and thresholds were lowered from five to two-and-a-half billion ECU.

Under the Merger Regulation, DG IV makes the first attempt to accommodate the special status of the media industry within existing EU competition law. Member states are permitted under Article 21 of the Merger Regulation, which stipulates that national authorities may protect legitimate interests, to enact national legislation to preserve media pluralism. DG IV regards these pluralism cases as originating either when separately defined markets are involved in multi-media transactions or when media mergers, which are not viewed as a threat to competition, are perceived as a danger to pluralism.

What are the core arguments and beliefs buttressing the use of competition policy in media policy? It is useful to examine the constraints that DG IV has to overcome in order to be active in the media industry. The idea of national media concentration legislation is to provide for a large number of players in the market in order to ensure media pluralism. DG IV cannot justify its rulings on these grounds, as it has no legal basis. DG IV – to illustrate with an example – can intervene in the market when there is abuse of dominant position, but cannot use the argument of cultural diversity for impeding a merger. This is because the EU has no jurisdiction in cultural policy (which continues to be protected by the principle of subsidiarity), there is yet no directive for media concentration and the European Court of Justice – as will be seen below – has identified the media industry as a service (and therefore equal to other industrial sectors under competition law). On balance, DG IV has to follow a very narrow path when taking decisions about media. The path is made narrower by the fact that many media mergers fall short of the Merger Regulation's turnover thresholds.

However, DG IV has defined media markets more narrowly as to be able to justify recommendations and decisions on the basis of dominant position criteria. Once the markets are defined narrowly, it is possible to take decisions which, although based on economic criteria, have the ultimate effect of safeguarding pluralism. In the February 1990 Communication (*Communication to the Council and European Parliament on Audio-visual Policy*[21]), DG IV identifies the audio-visual sector as being different to other sectors due to a number of 'specific economic and cultural considerations'.[22] EU competition rules would continue to apply equally to the audio-visual sector as they do to other sectors, but a list of factors relevant to the audio-visual sector were given which would be taken into consideration when media competition decisions are made. The 1990 Communication defines three distinct audio-visual markets: a) production and distribution of cinema and television films; b) the market for television broadcasts; and c) the market for satellite broadcasting services. In subsequent rulings on media mergers and acquisitions, DG IV has continued to further define separate product markets within these (above-mentioned) markets. Separate rulings have so far specified the following product markets: free access television (advertised), free access television (non-advertised), pay television, cable television, satellite broadcasting (general), and satellite broadcasting (wholly dedicated to sport).

Similar distinctions for newspaper markets have been made. DG IV divides the newspaper market into the market for newspaper readers and the market for newspaper advertising. The reader's market is then separated into trade publications, economic and financial magazines, women's magazines, television magazines, specialized amateur and professional magazines (motoring, travel, gardening, etc.) and daily newspapers. There are also distinctions made between quality and tabloid papers (Lang 1997).

Although DG IV did not look negatively upon cooperation between European media companies, it would ensure that programming material is not withdrawn from the market as a result. DG IV – in its official documents – further expresses concern that media companies may fix prices in the purchase of programming from third parties. Based upon Article 85, the Commission is also opposed to the joint acquisition or distribution of programming rights (although exemptions could be granted). Where exemptions were granted, and a multinational organization achieves joint exclusive rights for its members, non-members must be allowed access to programming. When exclusive programming rights are obtained, they cannot be of 'excessive' duration and later conditions cannot be added to the contract. These considerations are to apply to both public and private media companies.

It is not necessary to describe the details of this strategy (Harcourt 1999). Suffice it to mention that DG IV has been able to take decisions in a growing number of media cases. Out of a total of ten negative decisions on mergers taken by DG IV since 1989, seven pertain to the media industry. The key instrument assisting the launch of this interventionist strategy has been the narrow definition of media markets. By dividing and segmenting the media markets into narrower and narrower terms, DG IV has found enough room to employ standard EU competition policy.

However, there are limits to this strategy. First, DG IV is understaffed and the growth of media cases is placing an increasing burden upon scarce human resources. Second, technological convergence is blurring the definition of the media market. For DG IV, this is a serious challenge because its strategy has been one of defining markets in narrow terms. But if convergence re-expands the media market, DG IV will be left with Penelope's wedding veil! What DG IV does in the day, technology undoes at night. Third, DG IV is treading a difficult path, and its exercise would be made easier, in abstract, by the existence of a directive targeted towards the peculiarities of media ownership policy.

But it is at this point that the turf battle with DG XV begins. In abstract terms, DG IV could have an easier job – should a directive on media ownership be submitted and approved. However, DG IV has been able to secure a limited yet exclusive terrain for its initiatives and does not wish to surrender to the 'monopoly' of DG XV in media policy. As shown by other studies (Cini 1996; Harcourt 1998; see also Chapter Three) the different DGs of the Commission have developed their own administrative cultures and often compete against each other when the control of the Commission's agenda is at stake. For this reason DG IV has not been a traditional ally of DG XV. At the political level, the different Commissioners (van Miert and Monti) have closed most of the gap between them (as illustrated by Harcourt 1999), but a degree of hostility between the two services remain. All in all, the very day that DG IV agrees to Monti's proposal for a directive on media policy, it will offer the control of the agenda to DG XV and waste the capital of policy initiatives cumulated throughout the recent years.

This explains why a bone of contention between DG XV and DG IV is the choice of policy instruments. As explained above, DG XV's favoured option is audience share. This instrument does not fit well with competition law because the Merger Regulation does not contemplate audience share. For DG IV, accordingly, audience share represents an attempt to bring the regulation of the media industry further and further away from its policy domain. Hence the confrontation between the two DGs on policy instruments. Audience share makes media policy unique and inherently different from classic competition policy. It would be impossible to talk about audience share in the context of, say, competition in the chemical industry! By contrast, when turnover is employed, the media industry can be treated in the same way as the chemical industry. Interestingly, the choice of a policy instrument instead of another reflects competition between different DGs over the policy agenda.

Turning to the European Court of Justice (ECJ), what is the input given by this institution to the emergence of the governance regime? The ECJ has taken many decisions concerning broadcasting and the press (Harcourt 1999). To begin with, the ECJ has established the legitimacy of EU action in this field through a series of rulings precedent to the TWF directive. The thorny question was whether media policy should be considered part and parcel of national cultural policy, and therefore exempted from EU competition law and single market initiatives, or not. The response of the ECJ has been that broadcasting is a tradeable service like any other. According to the Court, a television signal must be considered a provision of services. Consequently, discrimination by a member state against a broadcasting signal due to its national origin is illegal. With these principles established, the Commission has been able to put forward the liberalizing infrastructure of TWF. Unsurprisingly then, TWF refers to the ECJ jurisprudence as providing legitimacy to EU media policy.

Moreover, the ECJ has assessed the status of public broadcasters and the social responsibility doctrine. The view of the ECJ is that public broadcasters should not be exempted from EU competition law. Hence there is no need to guarantee particular opt-outs in the name of the public service paradigm. This principle paves the way to the massive application of competition law against public monopoly in the national media industry. However, the protocol to the Amsterdam Treaty goes in the opposite direction of preserving the special status of public broadcasters. It remains to be seen whether and how will the protocol be implemented. Clearly, there is a degree of tension between the ECJ view and the Treaty protocol.

Concluding on the ECJ, it has contributed to the emergence of the governance regime in two ways. First, the ECJ has subtracted media policy from national cultural policy, and placed it within the policies of the EU. Second, the ECJ has found that public service broadcasters should be considered equivalent to commercial broadcasters. Overall, the impact of the ECJ has been profound and directed towards liberalization.

Policy instruments and policy diffusion

In analogy with the previous chapters, process tracking is suspended in this section and attention is turned to technocratic legitimacy.

This will be done by drawing upon the conceptual framework of policy diffusion introduced in Chapter Three. In the cases of the single currency and tax policy, the existence of national models to be imitated has been an important pre-condition for the making of EU policy. One of the reasons at the root of EMU is the presence of the German model of monetary policy. Tax policy does not exhibit a similar centre of gravity. *Coeteris paribus*, this has made policy diffusion more problematic. What about media regulation? The debate on EU policy instruments started without the benchmark provided by national models to be imitated and diffused. Did this constrain the legitimacy of EU action in this area? Let us proceed with order.

As averred, the EU media concentration policy process has witnessed a persistent attempt of the Commission to finalize a draft proposal. The European Parliament has endorsed the issue of EU rules. Yet European institutions have been facing numerous hurdles. As explained above, media ownership regulation touches upon fundamental issues of pluralism and cultural identity. The legitimacy of EU institutions is severely constrained. Suffice it to say that the EU is bereft of a right (with constitutional status) to freedom of expression, which (in Germany, Italy and other countries) is the most important foundation for national media concentration legislation. However, as mentioned earlier, EU media ownership policy has made progress, although it is still in the early stage of agenda setting. Isomorphism (the tendency to become alike, see Chapter Three) has been instrumental in this advancement of the governance regime, but in a very unconventional way. Indeed, the Commission, by suggesting the adoption of certain policy instruments in national legislation, created the pre-conditions for policy diffusion.

The choice of policy instruments is the crucial element. As illustrated above, the most innovative component of EU proposals is its stress on audience share as the key instrument for measuring the strength of media companies. The Commission, in its second Green Paper on media concentration regulation, was the first to suggest this utilization of audience share measurement as the most appropriate policy instrument. Interestingly, both in the UK and in Germany the Commission's idea of audience share measurement for media concentration found favourable reception among national policy makers who were revising domestic rules. In Germany, the 1996 interstate treaty restricts broadcasters to thirty per cent of audience share. In the UK, a new market measurement was introduced in the 1996 Broadcasting Act to limit audience share of broadcasters to fifteen per cent.

Why were national policy makers so keen on taking on board the Commission's suggestion? Presumably, policy instruments affect the position of different actors in the policy process and consequently attention must be turned to the relationship between instruments and actors. In the UK, the utilization of audience share – a 'cultural' measure, as opposed to more 'economic' indicators and measures – has strengthened the grip of the then Department of National Heritage (now Department of Culture, Media and Sport) on media ownership regulation. Other measures would have shifted the control of agenda from this Department to the Department of Trade and Industry. For example, regulating media through market shares (or revenue shares) assigns media concentration policy the status of a *sui generis* competition policy. Inter-bureaucratic competition for agenda control (between the Department of National Heritage and the Department of Trade and Industry) is the crucial factor which brought about the adoption of this apparently innocuous instrument of regulation in the UK. By buying suggestions from Brussels, national bureaucracies hence became implicitly involved in the early stage of EU policy diffusion. Similarly, in Germany the choice of audience share ensured that the jurisdiction of media concentration policy remained with the Länder (state) governments, which are constitutionally responsible for cultural policy concerns, and was not transferred to the federal government's cartel office (*Bundeskartellamt*).

Once audience share measure entered the UK and German political debate, the Commission turned to its congenial role of catalysing diffusion processes. Indeed, the Commission is now arguing that its announced directive is nothing but the extension of national regulatory instruments to the EU level. The UK and German governments, which are the only EU member states not to have endorsed the competence of the Commission in this area, may therefore be shooting themselves in the foot by adopting precisely the policy instrument suggested by the Commission in its two Green Papers. Diffusion of the audience share model in national legislation makes it easier for the Commission to propose EU legislation based upon this policy instrument. The case of media ownership regulation should not be over-emphasized: all in all, this EU policy process is at its initial stage, with a directive announced but not formally submitted. However, media regulation shows that technocratic legitimacy in the EU politics is not a constant, but a variable resource that can be created with *ad hoc* 'insemination' of instruments to be transferred.

Conclusion: a non-technocratic governance regime?

The EU embarked on media ownership regulation by relying on the typical arguments for harmonization (the level playing field argument), technical considerations on the future of the media industry, and the logic of the single market. A major preoccupation of the Commission was the avoidance of broader concerns of democracy. Technocratic legitimacy has been buttressed by the entrepreneurial action of the Commission. Models have been devised in Brussels, then adopted in Germany and the UK, and have been eventually recommended as EU policy instruments.

The governance regime that has ensued, however, is quite different from a purely technocratic ideal-type. A governance regime can be examined by looking at its participants, their beliefs, the policy outcomes, and the balance between negative and positive integration. In terms of participants, the media ownership policy process has been gradually structured around three main coalitions of actors, portrayed in Table 6.1.[23] Three coalitions compete for the control of this governance regime. They can be identified by their approach to EU policy making. The single market coalition – headed by DG XV – argues for harmonization of national ownership rules across a single EU measure of concentration. Concentration should be measured according to audience share across media (for example, by taking into account cross-ownership of TV, radio stations, and the press). The proposed directive presented by Commissioner Monti on several occasions – but never agreed by the College of Commissioners – would be along the lines of the single market approach. Reflecting a learning process, the purpose of the 'single market' coalition has evolved to the point of taking on board some of the concerns presented by the advocates of pluralism and cultural diversity (that is, by the coalition for pluralism).

The second coalition has found its champion in the European Parliament. Within the Commission, DG X has been supportive of an approach based on the appreciation of the diversity and cultural

Table 6.1 *Advocacy coalitions in the EU media ownership policy process*

	Single market	Pluralism	Convergence
Pivotal actor	DG XV	European Parliament	DG XIII
Other members	■ Some German Länder ■ France (recently, for tactical reasons) ■ Commissioner for Competition Policy	■ DG X ■ Regions ■ Public interest groups ■ International Federation of Journalists ■ Public broadcasters ■ French Minister of Culture	■ DG III ■ DG IV ■ DG I ■ ECJ ■ OECD ■ WTO ■ USA ■ Large media groups ■ German federal government ■ UK
Approach to EU policy	■ Harmonization of domestic laws around a single European rule ■ Audience share as main policy instrument	■ Limits to liberalization ■ Opt-out for public broadcasters ■ Defence of pluralism and cultural diversity	■ Liberalization ■ Policy convergence ■ Use of EU competition policy

matters of media policy. Public interest groups such as federations of consumers and journalists are typical members of the pluralist coalition. According to the second coalition, media policy is inherently different from the other goods and services traded in the single market. As it touches upon fundamental freedoms, it should be governed by a distinctive regime, based on cultural policy considerations and on democracy as the ultimate yardstick. Member states that are particularly worried about the future of public television and the role of the *service public* – such as France – have traditionally joined this coalition. However, given the rising influence and power of the third coalition (that is, the coalition for 'convergence'), members of the pluralist coalition see the initiatives of DG

XV as an acceptable second best. This explains why the French government is tactically supporting Commissioner Monti.

A third coalition – labelled the 'convergence' coalition and headed by DG XIII – is gaining increasing power in the EU policy process, the reason being the dominance of the 'information society' in the EU agenda. So much so that even Commissioner Monti has sought to re-present his initiative as complementary to the information society. Media policy – the advocates of convergence argue – is a component of a broader technological drive towards convergence. It would be foolish to establish boundaries between media and other technologies such as telecommunications and the internet. EU policy should assist the growth of the information society by providing an ultimately liberalizing policy. The EU should switch from media policy to broader technology policy, and consequently DG XIII should control the agenda, not DG XV.

As it has been very difficult to conceptualize media ownership policy solely in terms of the single market, the coalition for convergence wishes to absorb it into the information society framework. One difference between the first and the third coalition is that harmonization of media ownership policy guarantees the continued existence of media regulatory authorities at the national level, whereas convergence policy requires the abolishment of these authorities which are accounting for 'over-regulation'. The basic idea of convergence is to regulate all media equally. The single market initiative of Commissioner Monti, instead, distinguishes between telecommunications and media industries, defines print, radio and television broadcasting and new service markets separately, and distinguishes between public and private companies.

The coalition for convergence comprises of member states which, for various reasons, are opposed to a directive on media concentration and prefer not to isolate media issues from the Commission's agenda for the information society. Germany and the UK are two points in case, although Germany, being a federal political system with cultural policy assigned to the Länder, exhibits different positions at the sub-national level.[24] The coalition links EU policy and wider international agendas as indicated by the presence of DG I alongside DG XIII. DG XIII aims to fuse EU policy on the information society with the transatlantic initiative on the 'global information society'. This goal is appreciated by DG I.

The position of DG IV in this coalition is a bit awkward. DG IV has contributed to the emergence of the media governance regime, most distinctively by segmenting media markets. In itself, this operation acknowledges, at least implicitly, the cultural dimension and the peculiarities of the media industry. It is also not very different from Commissioner Monti's approach to define markets as precisely as possible. This should make it easier to find a terrain of collaboration between DG IV and DG XV. However, the reality shows a low level of cooperation between the two DGs, although at the political level the respective Commissioners are closer. Indeed, van Miert is close to Monti's position, as indicated in Table 6.1, even if DG XV and DG IV remain somewhat distant, essentially for reasons of bureaucratic politics.

Concluding on adversarial coalitions, the level of conflict is so high that it has been impossible to agree on a formal proposal to be submitted by the Commission to the other EU institutions. Elements of learning have facilitated the dialogue between the single market coalition and the pluralist coalition, but the emergence of the advocates of convergence adds complexity to the decision-making process. It would be erroneous, however, to assess the governance regime only by reference to the proposed directives. In terms of policy outcomes the governance regimes should be examined by including the activity of DG IV and the jurisprudence of the ECJ. DG IV has introduced a number of original elements of EU media policy by progressing along the narrow path provided by standard EU competition policy. Similarly to what happened in other regulatory policies, the ECJ has been left with the 'increasingly difficult task of reconciling the demands of integration with the desire to protect valued regulatory goals' (Armstrong and Bulmer 1998: 267–8). For the time being, the ECJ has impressed a clear liberalizing turn to the governance regime. As a result, the progress in negative integration has been immensely greater than the progress in positive integration. However, the negative decisions taken by DG IV (against mergers of media companies) and the protocol to the Amsterdam Treaty reflect an increasing demand for positive integration. Should a directive proceed according to the beliefs of the single market coalition, this would be a further crucial element of positive integration.

An important characteristic of the governance regime is the ideational dimension. The three adversarial coalitions support different beliefs and advance diverse arguments. More generally, my point is that technocratic arguments have been present both in the single market and in the convergence coalition, but they have not been uncontested. Democracy, pluralism, freedom of the press, and other non-technocratic arguments have now entered the debate. Whatever shape should a directive on media ownership take, the European Parliament has now developed enough institutional capacity to contrast technocracy in the EU media policy process. And the parliament is not alone. 'Common interest' pressure groups have been mobilized and have politicized the debate both at the EU level and in most of the member states. Countries such as France are eager to defend the *service public*, although one should bear in mind that, in the past, governments have defended the political control of the media (not pluralism!) in the name of the *service public*. Finally, the single market coalition has modified its beliefs as to include pluralist themes in its proposal, as illustrated above. There is evidence, therefore, that learning across coalitions has led to a modification of the single market coalition's secondary beliefs.[25]

Intertwined to mobilization is the question as to whether media ownership policy has been processed in relative isolation (the 'pillarization' question introduced above). Fragmentation is a classic manifestation of bureaucratic politics. If media policy has not been captured by technocratic policy making, is it predestined to be subsumed under bureaucratic politics? My answer is . . . no and yes! No, because both for technological reasons and for the increasingly wider debate, media policy has expanded beyond its original pillars. Yes, however, because there are clear indications of another dimension of bureaucratic politics (apart from pillarization), that is, intra-bureaucratic battles. As mentioned in Chapter Three, bureaucratic politics implies that 'the actors will strive to preserve their own powers, perhaps even if it means reducing the capacity of the resulting arrangements to make "good" policy for the Community as a whole' (Peters 1992: 118). In the case of media ownership regulation, competition for power has reached the level of individual DGs. The distance between DG IV and DG XV can be explained only in terms of different bureaucratic structures fighting for the control of the Commission's agenda and the protection of their respective policy territories. The conflict inside the College of Commissioners is an astonishing example of bureaucratic politics and its paralysing effects. Actors strive to preserve their power even when the cost is to expose internal conflict and the renounce to a formal proposal sustained by the whole College.

This consideration brings us to the last question introduced above, that is, what is the role of the Commission in this policy process? Frankly, it is impossible to analyse the Commission as a unitary actor. An actor is an individual or a collective body which has a unique and consistent set of objectives. The fact that different DGs belong to adversarial coalitions is revealing of the lack of unique goals within the Commission. The most interesting point is another, however. Not only has the politicization of EU media regulation been exacerbated by the split inside the Commission, but anti-technocratic discourse and policy have originated from DG X (in close alliance with the European Parliament). Thus the body who supposedly incarnates technocracy (the Commission) has been the cradle of the anti-technocratic challenge!

In conclusion, media ownership regulation does not fit in neatly with one of the four categories introduced in Chapter Three (technocracy, bureaucratic politics, epistemic communities and political decision making). A candidate to be excluded is epistemic communities. Policy makers are not facing a situation where they puzzle over their interests and communities of experts assist (or provide) the definition of preferences. Bureaucratic politics, by contrast, are very much alive in this policy area, but do not tell the whole story. Political decision making is making progress, after starting under the aegis of technocracy (as witnessed by the inception of the discussion on TWF). As for the future, the increasing importance of the information society in the Commission's agenda could tilt the process towards technocratic regulation, although politicization, once triggered, does not disappear easily. Judging by the current situation, I would argue that media ownership regulation contains elements of both bureaucratic politics and politicization, with the shadow of technocracy still lurking upon the future.

Notes

1 For a more rigorous introduction to alternative normative theories of the media see the classic Siebert *et al.* (1956) and McQuail (1994: chapter 5). The reader will note that my usage of the term pluralism in this section is not limited to the existence of different players (public and private) in the media markets, but entails the active

participation of citizens (Keane 1992). Also, with 'benign technocracy' I refer to the possible distortions of the social responsibility doctrine, to be outlined briefly below. With this I do not want to place any derogatory emphasis on the social responsibility doctrine. Simply, I intend to stress that it corresponds to a view of politics which puts a premium on governments steering society, rather than the other way round.

2 On the development of the media industry and regulatory policies across European countries see Humphreys (1996). The development of the European media industry is illustrated by Sanchez-Tabernero *et al.* (1993). On EU media ownership regulation see Harcourt (1998; 1999) and Beltrame (1996).

3 The public service model as outlined by Blumler has been questioned by a new emphasis on citizens as free consumers and on their demand, as opposed to the previous policy of supply (Wolton 1992). For a description of this paradigmatic shift and the intellectual mood of the 1980s see Hoffmann-Riem (1986) and the volume edited by Veljanovski (1989) for the pro-market think tank Institute of Economic Affairs.

4 There has been constant pressure for the abolition of the public broadcasting monopoly from this lobby, keen on expanding its market. See Mattelart and Palmer (1991).

5 For example, a TV company integrates vertically when it decides to produce directly programmes and films.

6 On concentration in the press see Humphreys (1996: chapter 3).

7 In the reconstruction of EU media policy I draw upon extensive research conducted by Alison Harcourt under the aegis of the ESRC project entitled *Regulating for media pluralism: issues in competition and ownership* (reference L126251009). The results of her research have now been published in her Ph.D dissertation (Harcourt 1999). I wish to thank Alison Harcourt for her collaboration: she is the author of this and the next two sections.

8 PEDOC A2-102/85, 30.09.85.

9 PEDOC A2-246/87, 08.12.87 (in which the European Parliament suggested two 1987 amendments for media concentration to the draft Directive TWF).

10 As envisaged by the European Parliament, pluralism refers to a situation wherein competition among a plurality of market players is accompanied by a public service catering for non-commercial goals. Pluralism also yields rules on content, cultural diversity, and respect of minorities and regional identities.

11 The 1990 De Vries Report 'Resolution on media concentration' (OJC 68 19/3/90) called for the Commission to counteract the growing trend towards media concentration in Europe (PEDOC A3-293/294/ 90, 15.02.90); in February 1990 the EP presented a related Resolution on freedom of the press; in September 1991 the EP released a working paper *Media concentration and diversity of opinion in Europe* which concluded that 'competition law is not a substitute for media law' and suggested laws for concentration, a European monitoring body, and a media code; a further 'Resolution on media concentration and pluralism of information' 1992 called for harmonization of national media regulations and the protection of pluralism (PEDOC A3-153/92, 16.09.92).

12 COMM (92) 480 'Pluralism and media concentration in the internal market' 23.12.92.

13 The European Parliament Resolution (1994) 'Pluralism and media concentration' A3-0435/93 was in favour of harmonization.

14 The Economic and Social Committee (1993) 'Opinion on Commission Green Paper' 93/C 304/07 was also in favour of harmonization.

15 These were simply: 1. no action; 2. transparency action; and 3. harmonization action.

16 The TWF provision for European content has been consistently bombarded by US representatives to the WTO table and Brussels as a barrier to trade. In an interview with *European Voice* 25–31.07.96, US representative to the EU, Vernon Weaver, states 'I will not be shy about defending key US industries, such as the audio-visual industry, against new protectionist measures, however packaged.'

17 PEDOC A3-435/93, 05.01.94.

18 COM (94) 353 final, 05.10.94, 'Follow up to the consultation process relating to the Green Paper on "Pluralism and media concentration in the internal market" – an assessment of the need for Community action'.

19 See Harcourt (1999) for details.

20 Council Regulation 4064/89, OJL 395/1, 1989, amended by OJL 257/14, 1990.

21 COM(90) 78 final, 21.02.90.

22 These, the Communication claims, relate to the structural weakness of the audio-visual sector and to the high level of intra-sector cooperation.

23 I decided not to plot member states on the Table (with a few exceptions), although most of them have preferences in terms of what the EU governance regime should be. The reason for this choice is that,

in the absence of a formal proposal of the Commission, member states have not discussed formally at the Council level.

24 Berlin, Saxony, Schleswig-Holstein, Hamburg, and North-Rhein Westphalia support Commissioner Monti, whereas Bayern and Thüringen join the German federal government in the convergence coalition.

25 Remember that deep core beliefs are similar to axioms or ideology, and accordingly tend to be rather unchangeable. Secondary beliefs are more permeable to learning dynamics (see Sabatier 1998 and Chapter Three).

CHAPTER SEVEN

Conclusions

A few years ago, a book edited by two Scandinavian political scientists (Andersen and Eliassen 1996) expressed concern about the evolution of the EU with the following title: *The European Union: how democratic is it?* This study has dealt with the symmetric question of 'How technocratic is the EU?' Technocracy is a complex concept. It was developed in the past century, and found a fertile terrain in the fascination for progress, technology and technical expertise typical of the early stages of capitalism. Technocracy has now changed into the politics of expertise (Fischer 1990). This transformation makes the concept of technocracy elusive. The situation is compounded by the fact that technocracy has both an ideological and an empirical content. In both senses, it remains a concept with many drawbacks, for the reasons illustrated in Chapter Two.

All the same, for the purposes of this study the concept of technocracy can be employed to shed light on those areas of EU public policy making dominated by high uncertainty and low political salience. Other types of EU policy are better captured by more modern concepts, namely bureaucratic politics and epistemic communities. At any rate, the analysis of the single currency, direct tax policy, and media ownership regulation show that the politics of expertise in its various forms is at work in the EU. Its power is enhanced by the potential technocratic bias of regulatory policies (see Chapter Two). The mechanisms of policy transfer (coercion, mimetism and normative pressure) enhance the power of expertise by providing a source of technocratic legitimacy. In this chapter the issue of technocratic legitimacy will be tackled first, before a general assessment of technocracy in the three areas under examination is presented. Finally, I will present my thoughts on the wider issues of technocracy, legitimacy and the democratization of the EU.

Technocratic legitimacy

Since the early writings on technocratic utopias, it has been recognized that the legitimacy of the 'government by experts' is a serious problem. In the past century, authors such as Comte claimed that a solution to this problem was to be found in the old, medieval distinction between spiritual and temporal power. Managers could seize temporal power, but scientists, artists, philosophers and intellectuals in general would provide the moral fabric of society. Therefore they would be entrusted with spiritual power. In modern, secularized, democratic political systems this dichotomization of power is not a viable solution to the contradictions of technocratic politics. In the case of the EU, the situation is compounded by the democratic deficit of its institutions. All the same, policy legitimacy in the narrow sense is achieved when a policy proposal goes through the various stages of the EU policy process and eventually is agreed upon by the Council of Ministers. In this narrow sense, a policy proposal made by the Commission is legitimized as EU public policy. This does not say much as to whether that proposal will meet the support of the citizens, will be efficient, will be perceived as based on procedural fairness, and will yield distributive fairness. For this reason I have used the notion of technocratic legitimacy, as opposed to wider forms of legitimacy (Banchoff and Smith 1998; Beetham and Lord 1998; Weatherford 1992).

The literature on policy transfer and imitation (or isomorphism, the tendency to become alike) sheds light on three main routes to technocratic legitimacy. As explained in Chapter Three, the three mechanisms of technocratic legitimacy are coercion, mimetism and normative pressures. What do the case studies of EMU, tax policy, and media ownership regulation show in this respect? EMU was achieved thanks to different elements: history and learning, bargaining, the anchor power of the Deutschmark, and the consensus on the paradigm of policy credibility. In terms of mechanisms of policy transfer, coercion, mimetism and normative pressures were instrumental in providing technocratic legitimacy. Coercion refers both to the anchor power of the Deutschmark in the European Monetary System, and to the pressure on domestic public finance induced by the convergence criteria. Mimetism is linked to uncertainty: the latter found a response in the imitation of the (perceived) most successful national model of monetary policy. Normative pressures are typified by the Delors Committee. This Committee shaped the EMU policy process in accordance with the shared beliefs and values of the central bankers.

On balance, however, mimetism was the most powerful mechanism in EMU. The Commission hence is more an efficient catalyst in the diffusion of existing models than the designer of new models. Taxation seems to confirm the assertion that when EU institutions cannot catalyse mimetic process (because there is no national tax policy model deemed optimal and therefore suitable for imitation) technocracy comes to an impasse. So much so that the Commission has sought to re-focus the debate in political (as opposed to technocratic) terms. However, media concentration suggests a crucial qualification in that it shows how the Commission – to a certain extent – can devise policy instruments that are first purposefully inseminated in member states and then proposed for isomorphic diffusion to the whole of the EU.

Let me be more precise. Judging from the cases of EMU and tax policy, the conclusion would be that the presence of desirable national models is a necessary[1] condition for technocratic legitimacy. But this conclusion is flawed: the picture changes as soon as one considers the third case study (media ownership policy). The third case study provides two lessons. First, however important a national model may be, it does not represent a necessary condition for policy transfer. The Commission has been able to set the agenda for EU media ownership policy without drawing upon lessons provided endogenously by member states. Second, when there are no models, diffusion processes can be triggered by the strategic construction of national examples, as shown by insemination of policy instruments in media ownership regulation. Bearing in mind Offe's observation that design is often presented as imitation even when it is creation (Offe 1992), the strategy pursued by the Commission makes political sense. For a policy entrepreneur acting in the constrained EU political system, the dissemination of best practices and models is an efficient strategy for building technocratic legitimacy. The Commission cannot be accused of trying to impose 'the view of Brussels' if it follows a policy design that is already in place somewhere in the EU . . . no matter if that national policy design was originally inspired by Brussels!

The politicization of the EU policy process

In conclusion, the puzzle of lack of democratic legitimacy and increasing activity of the EU can be explained by considering isomorphism as a political strategy. The Commission, acting as an entrepreneurial actor, exploits the political properties of isomorphism and, under the conditions explored above, can secure 'technocratic' legitimacy, that is, a type of legitimacy confined to the formal hurdles to be leapt over in the EU policy process. The mechanisms of policy transfer are in turn enhanced by the supply and demand of regulation as investigated in Chapter Three (see also Majone 1996).

Technocracy is a challenge, but it is not overwhelming. To begin with, expertise is not confined to technocracy. Epistemic communities have been influential in the EMU design and occasionally in tax policy, and bureaucratic politics pervades media ownership policy. Secondly, in the three cases under examination the power of technocracy, bureaucratic politics, and epistemic communities has been ultimately counterbalanced by a process of politicization. Case studies do not allow for statistical generalization, yet they have potential for theoretical development (Yin 1994).[2] Of the three cases, EMU provides the clearest example of the power of economic ideas and non-elected policy experts and professionals. Yet even in the EMU case it would be a mistake to argue that political decision making was kept at bay by epistemic communities or economic policy paradigms. Quite the contrary, political factors played a large role, and ultimately prevailed over the politics of expertise.

Tax policy illustrates how the Commission itself can force stalemate by switching from technocratic policy to a more political discussion on harmful tax competition. The recent progress made in this policy area can be ascribed, indeed, to a renewed political interest in tax coordination. Left to technocratic debates on the efficiency of the European tax systems, EU direct tax policy would have never gone further than minimal measures. As averred, the most interesting feature of the EU tax policy process is that bureaucrats (that is, the Commission) demand political decisions rather than technocracy.

Media ownership regulation supplies yet another manifestation of the politics of expertise. Technocratic arguments are present in two of the three coalitions fighting for the control of this governance regime. In similarity with tax policy, epistemic communities are not a major actor in media policy. By contrast, technocracy and bureaucratic politics have been present throughout the evolution of the governance regime described in Chapter Six. All the same, the most striking feature is the gradual politicization of the debate on EU media regulation. Political decision making is making progress. In conclusion, the three cases under examination presented the ideal prerequisites for the development of technocracy in terms of regulatory policy making, lack of an attentive public, and the level of expertise needed to handle these issues. Yet they are heading towards politicization, not towards the unbridled power of expertise.

The future: integrating expertise and democracy

Democratic legitimacy, however, raises wider issues. In this connection, one recommendation arising out of this study concerns the necessity to integrate expertise into the projects for a more democratic and legitimate Union. The EU is a political system where expertise matters considerably, arguably more than in domestic politics. The presence of bureaucratic politics, epistemic communities, technocratic public policy making is not unique to the EU. But the specialization of the EU in regulatory policy making accentuates the thorny issue of integrating technocracy and democracy. The solution devised by national political systems in the previous centuries – that is, strengthening the role of parliaments in the control of the executive – cannot be a panacea for the EU. Of course, the European Parliament has been extremely influential in recent EU policy developments. In the case of media ownership policy, the European Parliament has been instrumental in bringing pluralism back in the debate. Further, in tax policy it has endorsed the politicization of the initiatives against tax competition. In the future, the European Parliament will seek to raise its voice in EU macro-economic policy, by arguing that the European Central Bank should not be left in splendid isolation when crucial economic decisions are taken. Thus the European Parliament has considerable potential as an agent of democratization, especially if a European *demos* and a European identity will materialize soon. Yet the EU needs to strengthen the accountability and the responsiveness of its whole institutional network. Strengthening one player against the others could be wrong. One of the authors who has studied the bureaucratization of the EU policy process in great detail, Edward Page, has concluded that:

> Bringing more players into the system, whether through a stronger role for the European Parliament or national or regional legislatures and, perhaps even more importantly, their staffs, might not reduce the democratic deficit. Increasing the range of interests and bodies that have to be squared might increase the difficulty of identifying accountability, turning a democratic deficit into a less democratic surfeit of institutions, groups, and individuals, all with some sort of valid claim to represent European citizens. (Page 1997: 163)

Democratic control and accountability are concepts in search of new meanings even at the national level. Indeed, parliaments are facing increasing challenges in national political systems, where the traditional functions of redistribution have been accompanied (and to a certain extent superseded) by the growth of the regulatory state. The proliferation of non-majoritarian institutions (such as independent central banks and regulatory agencies) and networks of private and public actors have led authors such as Andersen and Burns (1996) to speak of post-parliamentary governance. The EU constitutes a peculiar accentuation of this trend, given the dense regulatory networks and the emphasis on efficiency (Dehousse 1997; Joerges *et al.* 1997; Majone 1996). This problematic situation requires a leap forward, rather than a journey back to the past of parliamentary control. In perspective, the increasing role played by politicization over expertise – as shown by the three studies presented in this book – is indicative of a positive maturation of the EU. Politics generates conflict, structures cleavages, and polarizes public opinion but at the same time frees the EU from the trap of technocracy. Democracy is all about conflict, and perhaps a certain degree of inefficiency in the policy process is the price that has to be paid for a wider participation and a more mature debate, as the case of media ownership regulation typifies. Politics can also force the impasse of technocratic policy making: the challenge of tax competition can be addressed only by shifting the policy discourse to the political level, not by recurring to sterile technocratic approaches. And the Euro will not transform Europe into the Garden of Eden by dint of its intrinsic technocratic virtue. Rather, the European Central Bank will be asked to take political decisions, such as whether to respond to the problem of unemployment with lower interest rates or not.

Politicization, in short, aids the maturation of the EU as a polity, and perhaps it will make it less different from national political systems. All the same, the problem of controlling regulatory bureaucracies and policy experts will not be solved automatically as time goes by. The question is not if and when the 'mandarins of Europe' will be substituted by democracy – no doubt that expertise in the EU is here to stay – but whether and how EU public policy will become more accountable. The conclusion of this book is not that technocracy has disappeared by the EU, but that expertise is operating in an increasingly politicized environment.

Much ground is still to be covered. Decision-making procedures were made more complex by the Treaty on the European Union, and the Treaty of Amsterdam has not brought about considerable progress. We are facing a paradoxical situation. On the one hand, growing complexity of decision-making processes can reduce EU legitimacy. On the other, the democratic deficit creates a heightened need to seek the broadest possible consensus among Commission, European Parliament and Council. In turn, this creates complexity, poor transparency, incomprehensibility of processes, and finally erodes the legitimacy of European action (Beetham and Lord 1998; Schmitter 1998).

However, the problem goes beyond the decision-making procedures and invests the essence of the EU. Various authors have proposed different solutions (Andersen and Burns 1996; Majone 1996: chapter 13; Schmitter 1998). From the particular perspective chosen for this study, the main recommendation is that technocracy should be taken seriously and accordingly solutions should face the specificity of EU public policies.[3] A policy process based on expertise, on the one hand, and a more politicized context, on the other, can be either an explosive combination or a corroborating alchemy, if the threat of technocracy is converted into the positive input of expertise in complex policy making. In this respect, the EU should look more at the best practices of regulatory reforms and regulatory management (OECD 1997) rather than at the past, that is, at the heyday of parliamentary control. A diffuse culture of accountability, procedural legitimacy,[4] the expertise and credibility of EU regulators, healthy competition among different regulatory bodies, the improvement of consultation and judicial review should provide the macro-trajectories (Majone 1996). At the micro level of instruments, the quality of the EU policy process could benefit from regulatory impact analysis, regulatory budgets and the systematic use of policy evaluation within a new culture of democracy by results (Radaelli 1998; Radaelli and Dente 1996). A more responsive and responsible Union is feasible, and the process of politicization could assist, rather than hinder, this development. Whether this will become reality depends on the institutions of the EU, but also on the priorities that national political leaders will assign to EU affairs, on less parochial patterns of education and socialization, and ultimately on the growth of an attentive public. I hope that this book will be part of this growing awareness.

Notes

1 Albeit not sufficient. EMU was achieved at the end of a multi-faceted political process, as illustrated in Chapter Four, and tax policy was directed by a complex constellation of variables (Chapter Five).
2 Additionally, the tendency towards politicization is confirmed by broad studies of European integration in the 1990s (Hooghe and Marks 1997). Hix (1998: 42) lists a number of recent developments pointing to the politicization of the EU, such as the mobilization of citizens on EU issues and the EU-targeted activities of private groups, public interests and social movements. Kohler-Koch (1997) detects an increased lobbying activity directed towards the European Parliament. This is yet another example of politicization.
3 The Treaty of Amsterdam illustrates the maturation of the debate, by including provisions inspired by the regulatory model alongside traditional provisions based on the parliamentary model (Dehousse 1998).
4 Majone (1996: chapter 13) argues that procedural legitimacy implies, among other things, democratic procedures for the specification of the goals and power of the regulators, and the requirement that regulators provide reasons for their decisions. This giving-reasons requirement – contained in Article 190 of the Treaty of Rome – stimulates public participation, peer review, and a systematic use of public policy analysis. It also makes the regulator's decisions amenable to judicial review.

References

Aaron, H.J. (1978) *Politics and the professors: the great society in perspective*, Washington: Brookings.

Aaron, H.J. (1989) 'Politics and the professors revisited', *American Economic Review* **79**(2) May: 1–15.

Adler, E. and Haas, P.M. (1992) 'Conclusion: epistemic communities, world order, and the creation of a reflective research program' in Haas, P.M. (ed.) 'Knowledge, power and international policy coordination', *International Organisation* Monographic Issue **46**(1): 367–90.

Adorno, T.W. (1941) 'Veblen's attack on culture', *Studies in Philosophy and Social Science* **9**: 389–413.

Akin, W.E. (1977) *Technocracy and the American dream. The Technocrat Movement, 1900–1941*, Berkeley: University of California Press.

Aldrich, H.E. (1979) *Organizations and environments*, Englewood Cliffs, N.J.: Prentice-Hall.

Alesina, A. (1989) 'Politics and business cycles in industrial democracies', *Economic Policy* **8**: 55–98.

Allison, G.A. (1971) *The essence of decision: explaining the Cuban Missile Crisis*, Boston: Little Brown.

Andersen, S.S. and Burns, T. (1996) 'The European Union and the erosion of parliamentary democracy: a study of post-parliamentary governance' in Andersen, S.S. and Eliassen, K.A. (eds) *The European Union: how democratic is it?*, Sage: London: 227–51.

Andersen, S.S. and Eliassen, K.A. (1996) (eds) *The European Union: how democratic is it?*, London: Sage.

Armstrong, K. and Bulmer, S. (1998) *The governance of the single market*, Manchester: Manchester University Press.

Banchoff, T. and Smith, M. (1998) *Legitimacy and the European Union*, Routledge: London.

Barker, R. (1990) *Political legitimacy and the state*, Oxford: Clarendon.

Barker, A. and Peters, G.B. (1992) (eds) *The politics of expert advice. Creating, using and manipulating scientific knowledge for public policy*, Pittsburgh: University of Pittsburgh Press.

157

Barrell, R. (1992) (ed.) *Economic convergence and monetary union in Europe*, London: Sage.

Barro, R. and Gordon, R. (1983) 'Rules, discretion and reputation in a model of monetary policy', *Journal of Monetary Economics* **12**: 101–22.

Beetham, D. (1991) *The legitimation of power*, London: Macmillan.

Beetham, D. and Lord, C. (1998) *Legitimacy*, Harlow: Longman.

Bell, D. (1960) *The end of ideology*, Glencoe: The Free Press.

Bell, D. (1973) *The coming of the post-industrial society*, New York: Basic Books.

Bellier, I. (1995) 'Une culture de la Commission Europeenne?' in Mény, Y., Muller, P. and Quermonne, J.L. (eds) *Politiques Publiques en Europe*, Paris: L'Harmattan: 49–60.

Beltrame, F. (1996) 'Harmonising media ownership rules: problems and prospects, *Utilities Law Review* **7**(5) September–October: 172–5.

Blumler, J. (1992) (ed.) *Television and the public interest. Vulnerable values in West-European broadcasting*, London: Sage.

Boston, J. (1988) 'Advising the prime minister in New Zealand: the origins, functions and evolution of the prime minister's advisory group', *Politics* **23**(1): 8–20.

Bovenberg, A.L. and de Jong, A.H.M. (1997) 'The road to economic and monetary union', *Kyklos* **50**(1): 83–109.

Breyer, S. (1982) *Regulation and its reform*, Cambridge (MA): Cambridge University Press.

Burnham, J. (1941) *The managerial revolution*, New York: John Day.

Burris, B. (1993) *Technocracy at work*, New York: State University of New York Press.

Cameron, D. (1995) 'Transnational relations and the development of European EMU' in Risse-Kappen, T. (ed.) *Bringing transnational relations back in*, Cambridge: Cambridge University Press: 37–78.

Caporaso, J. (1996) 'The European Union and forms of state: Westphalian, regulatory or post-modern?', *Journal of Common Market Studies* **34**(1) March: 29–52.

Carli, G. (1993) *Cinquant'anni di Vita Italiana* (Fifty years of Italian life), Bari: Laterza.

Cassese, S. and della Cananea, G. (1992) 'The Commission of the European Economic Community. The administrative ramifications of its political development (1957–1967)' in Heyen, E.V. (ed.) *Yearbook of European administrative history. Early European Community administration*, Baden-Baden: Nomos: 75–94.

Chirac, J. (1994) *La France Pour Tous*, Paris: Nil Editions.

Cini, M. (1996) 'La Commission Europeenne: Lieu d'emergence de cultures administratives. L'exemple de la DG IV et de la DG XI', *Revue Française de Science Politique* **46**(3) June: 457–72.

Coase, R.H. (1937) 'The nature of the firm', *Economica* 4: 385–405.

Coen, D. (1997) 'The evolution of the large firm as a political actor in the European Union', *Journal of European Public Policy* 4(1) March: 91–108.

Collingridge, D. and Reeve. C. (1986) *Science speaks to power. The role of experts in policy making*, London: Pinter.

Commission (1966) *The development of a European capital market (The Segre' Report)*, Brussels: EEC Commission.

Commission (1977) *Report of the study group on the role of public finance in European integration (MacDougall Report)*, Brussels: EEC Commission.

Commission (1992) *Report of the committee of independent experts on company taxation (The Ruding Report)*, Luxembourg: Office for Official Publications of the European Communities.

Commission (1996) *Taxation in the European Union: report on the development of tax systems*, COM (96) 546 Final.

Committee for the Study of Economic and Monetary Union (1989) *Report on Economic and Monetary Union in the European Community (Delors Report)*, Luxembourg: Office for Official Publications of the European Communities.

Coombes, D. (1970) *Politics and bureaucracy in the European Community. A portrait of the Commission of the EEC*, London: Allen & Unwin.

Council-Commission of the EC (1970) *Report to the Council and the Commission on the realization by stages of Economic and Monetary Union in the Community – Werner Report*, Brussels: Supplement to Bulletin 11–1970.

Cram, L. (1993) 'Calling the tune without paying the piper? Social policy regulation: the role of the Commission in European Community social policy', *Policy and Politics* 21(2): 135–46.

Crozier, M., Huntington, S. and Watanuki, J. (1975) *The crisis of democracy. Report on the governability of democracies to the Trilateral Commission*, New York: New York University Press.

Czarniawska, B. (1997) *Narrating the organization. Dramas of institutional identity*, Chicago and London: University of Chicago Press.

Dahl, R. (1985) *Controlling nuclear weapons. Democracy versus guardianship*, Syracuse, New York: Syracuse University Press.

Dahl, R. (1989) *Democracy and its critics*, New Haven: Yale University Press.

Dehousse, R. (1997) 'Regulation by networks in the European Community: the role of European agencies', *Journal of European Public Policy* 4(2) June: 246–61.

Dehousse, R. (1998) 'European institutional architecture after Amsterdam: parliamentary system or regulatory structure?,' *Robert Schuman Centre Working paper* no. 11/98, EUI: Florence.

Devereux, M. and Pearson, M. (1989) *Corporate tax harmonisation and economic efficiency*, London: IFS (Report Series no. 35).

DiMaggio, P. and Powell, W.W. (1991) 'The iron cage revisited: institutional isomorphism and collective rationality in organizational fields' in Powell, W.W. and DiMaggio, P. (eds) *The new institutionalism in organizational analysis*, Chicago: University of Chicago Press: 63–82.

Dogan, M. (1992) 'Conceptions of legitimacy' in Hawkesworth, M. and Kogan, M. (eds) *Encyclopaedia of government and politics*, London: Routledge: 116–26.

Dolowitz, D. and Marsh, D. (1996) 'Who learns from whom: a review of the policy transfer literature', *Political Studies* XLIV: 343–57.

Downs, A. (1967) *Inside bureaucracy*, Boston: Little, Brown.

Drake, H. (1997) 'The European Commission and the politics of legitimacy in the EU' in Nugent, N. (ed.) *At the heart of the Union. Studies of the European Commission*, London: Macmillan: 226–44.

Dyson, K. (1980) *The state tradition in Western Europe*, Oxford: Martin Robertson.

Dyson, K. (1994) *Elusive Union*, Harlow: Longman.

Dyson, K. and Featherstone, K. (1996a) 'Italy and EMU as vincolo esterno: empowering the technocrats, transforming the state', *South European Society and Politics* 1(2) Autumn: 272–99.

Dyson, K. and Featherstone, K. (1996b) 'EMU and economic governance in Germany', *German Politics* 5(3) December: 325–55.

Dyson, K. and Featherstone, K. (1997) 'Jacques Delors and the re-launch of EMU. A study of strategic calculation, brokerage and cognitive leadership', *Paper given to the 5th biennial international conference of ECSA*, 29 May–1 June, Seattle, USA.

Dyson, K. and Featherstone, K. (1999) *The Road to Maastricht: Negotiating the Maastricht Treaty*, Oxford: Oxford University Press.

Easson, A.J. (1993) *Taxation in the European Community*, London: The Athlone Press.

Egan, M. (1998) 'Regulatory strategies, delegation and European market integration', *Journal of European Public Policy* 5(3) September: 485–506.

Eichengreen, B. (1997) *European monetary unification. Theory, practice, and analysis*, Cambridge, Massachussets, and London: The MIT Press.

Eichengreen, B. and Frieden, J. (1993) 'The political economy of European monetary unification: an analytical introduction', *Economics and Politics* 5(2) July: 85–104.

Eichengreen, B. and Wyplosz, C. (1998) 'The stability pact: more than a minor nuisance?', *Economic Policy* 26 April: 67–113.

Eliassen, K.A. and Svaasand, L. (1975) 'The formation of mass political organisations: an analytical framework', *Scandinavian Political Studies* 10: 95–121.

Ellul, J. (1965) *The technological society*, London: Jonathan Cape.

Eulau, H. (1977) *Technology and civility. The skill revolution in politics*, Stanford: Hoover Institution.

Farmer, P. and Lyal, R. (1994) *EC tax law*, Oxford: Clarendon Press.

Featherstone, K. (1994) 'Jean Monnet and the democratic deficit in the EU', *Journal of Common Market Studies* 32(2) June: 149–70.

Ferkiss, V.C. (1969) *Technological man: the myth and the reality*, London: Heinemann.

Fischer, F. (1990) *Technocracy and the politics of expertise*, London: Sage.

Fischer, F. (1993) 'Policy discourse and the politics of Washington think tanks' in Fischer, F. and Forester, F. (eds) *The argumentative turn in policy analysis and planning*, London: UCL Press: 21–42.

Fisichella, D. (1997) *L'Altro Potere. Tecnocrazia e Gruppi di Pressione* (The other power. Technocracy and pressure groups), Rome-Bari (Italy): Laterza.

Foucault, M. (1980) *Power-knowledge – selected interviews and other writings 1972–1977*, edited by Colin Gordon, Hemel Hempstead: Prentice Hall.

Fratianni, M. and von Hagen, J. (1991) *The European Monetary System and European Monetary Union*, Boulder (CO): Westview.

Frenkel, J.A., Razin, A. and Sadka, E. (1991) *International taxation in an integrated world*, Cambridge: Cambridge University Press.

Friedman, M. (1968) 'The role of monetary policy', *American Economic Review* 58 March: 1–17.

Galbraith, J.K. (1967) *The New Industrial State*, Boston: Houghton Mifflin.

Garrett, G. (1993) 'The politics of Maastricht', *Economics and Politics* 5(2) July: 105–23.

Genschel, P. and Plümper, T. (1997) 'Regulatory competition and international cooperation', *Journal of European Public Policy* 4(4): 626–42.

George, S. (1995) 'The European Commission: opportunities seized, problems unresolved', *Paper presented to the biennial ECSA conference*, Charleston, South Carolina, May.

Giavazzi, F. and Pagano, M. (1988) 'The advantage of tying one's hand. EMS discipline and central bank credibility', *European Economic Review* 32(5) June: 1055–82.

Giavazzi, G., Micossi, S. and Milner, M. (1988) (eds) *The European Monetary System*, Cambridge: Cambridge University Press.

Goodhart, C. (1996) 'European monetary integration', *European Economic Review* 40: 1083–90.

Gormley, W.T. Jr. (1985–86) 'Regulatory issue-networks in a federal system', *Polity* (18): 595–620.

Gouldner, A. (1970) *The coming crisis of western sociology*, New York: Avon.

Gouldner, A. (1979) *The future of the intellectuals and the rise of a new class*, Oxford: Oxford University Press.

Grauwe, Paul de (1992) *The economics of monetary integration*, Oxford: Oxford University Press.

Grauwe, Paul de (1994) 'The need for real convergence in a monetary union' in Johnson, C. and Collignon, S. (eds) *The monetary economics of Europe*, London: Interpublishers: 269–79.

Grauwe, Paul de (1996) 'Monetary union and convergence criteria', *European Economic Review* 40: 1091–101.

Gray, V. (1973) 'Innovation in states: a diffusion study', *American Political Science Review* 67(4) December: 1174–85.

Haas, E. (1958) *The uniting of Europe*, Stanford: Stanford University Press.

Haas, P.M. (1992) (ed.) 'Knowledge, power and international policy co-ordination', *International Organisation* Monographic Issue, 46(1) Winter.

Habermas, J. (1970) *Toward a rational society*, Boston: Beacon Press.

Habermas, J. (1971) *Knowledge and human interests*, Boston: Beacon Press.

Hahn, H.J. (1998) 'The stability pact for European monetary union: compliance with deficit limit as a constant legal duty', *Common Market Law Review* 35(1) February: 77–100.

Hall, P. (1986) *Governing the economy. The politics of state intervention in Britain and France*, Cambridge: Polity Press.

Hall, P. (1989) (ed.) *The political power of economic ideas. Keynesianism across nations*, Princeton: Princeton University Press.

Hallerberg, M. and Basinger, S. (1998) 'Internationalization and changes in tax policy in OECD countries: the importance of domestic veto players', *Comparative Political Studies* 31(3) June: 321–52.

Harcourt, A. J. (1998) 'EU media concentration. The conflict over the definition of alternatives', *Journal of Common Market Studies* 36(3) September: 369–89.

Harcourt, A.J. (1999) 'European institutions and the media industry. European regulatory politics between pressure and pluralism', Ph.D. Dissertation, Department of Government, University of Manchester.

Heclo, H. (1972) 'Review article: policy analysis', *British Journal of Political Science* 2(1) January: 83–108.

Heclo, H. (1974) *Modern social politics in Britain and Sweden*, New Haven: Yale University Press.

Heritier, A. (1997) 'Policy-making by subterfuge: interest accommodation, innovation and substitute democratic legitimation in Europe – perspectives from distinctive policy areas', *Journal of European Public Policy* 4(2) June: 171–89.

Heyen, E.V. (1992) (ed.) *Yearbook of European administrative history. Early European Community administration*, Baden-Baden: Nomos.

Hix, S. (1998) 'The study of the European Union II: the "new governance" agenda and its rival', *Journal of European Public Policy* 5(1) March: 38–65.

Hoffmann-Riem, W. (1986) 'Law, politics, and the new media: trends in broadcasting regulation' in Dyson, K. and Humpheys, P. (eds) *The politics of the communications revolution in Western Europe*, London: Frank Cass: 125–46.

Hooghe, L. and Marks, G. (1997) 'The making of a polity. The struggle over European integration' in Kitschelt, H., Lange, P., Marks, G. and Stephens, J. (eds) *The politics and political economy of advanced industrial societies*, Cambridge: Cambridge University Press.

Humphreys, P. (1996) *Media and media policy in Western Europe*, Manchester: Manchester University Press.

IBFD – International Bureau of Fiscal Documentation (1963) *The EEC Reports on Tax Harmonization. The Reports of the Fiscal and Financial Committee and the Reports of the Sub-Groups A, B, and C*, Amsterdam: IBFD.

IFS – Institute for Fiscal Studies (1994) *Setting savings free. Proposals for the taxation of savings and profits*, London: IFS.

Joerges, C., Ladeur, K.H., and Vos, E. (1997) (eds) *Integrating scientific expertise into regulatory decision-making. National traditions and European innovations*, Baden-Baden: Nomos.

Kay, J. (1997) 'Evaluating the EMU criteria: theoretical constructs, member compliance and empirical testing', *Kyklos* **50**(1): 63–82.

Keane, J. (1991) *The media and democracy*, Cambridge: Polity.

Keane, J. (1992) 'Democracy and the media: without foundations', *Political Studies* **40**: 116–29.

Kingdon, J.W. (1984) *Agendas, alternatives and public policy*, Glenview, Illinois: HarperCollins.

Kohler-Koch, B. (1997) 'Organised interests and the European Parliament', *European Integration On-Line Papers*, http://eiop.or.at/.

Lang, J.T. (1997) *Media, multimedia and European Community antitrust law*, mimeograph, Brussels: Competition Directorate General of the European Commission.

Lange, P. (1993) 'Maastricht and the social protocol: why did they do it?', *Politics and Society* **21**(1) March: 5–36.

Lerner, D. and Lasswell, H. (1956) (eds) *The policy sciences*, Stanford: Stanford University Press.

Lewis-Beck, M. (1988) *Economics and elections. The major western democracies*, Ann Arbor, Michigan: University of Michigan Press.

Lindblom, C.E. (1959) 'The science of muddling through', *Public Administration* **19**: 78–88.

Lindblom, C.E. (1990) *Inquiry and change. The troubled attempt to understand and shape society*, New Haven: Yale University Press.

Locke, R. and Jacoby, W. (1997) 'The dilemmas of diffusion', *Politics and Society* **25**(1) March: 34–65.

Ludlow, P. (1982) *The making of the European Monetary System*, London: Butterworth.

Majone, G.D. (1990) (ed.) *Deregulation or re-regulation? Regulatory reform in Europe and the US*, New York: St. Martin's.

REFERENCES

Majone, G.D. (1996) (ed.) *Regulating Europe*, London: Routledge.

Marcussen, M. (1997) 'The role of ideas in the EMU-process: the case of three small economies and of European central bankers', *Paper prepared for presentation at the 5th biennial international conference of the European Community Studies Association*, 29 May–1 June, Seattle, USA.

Martin, L. (1993) 'International and domestic institutions in the EMU process', *Economics and Politics* 5(2) July: 125–145.

Matlary, J.H. (1997) 'Democratic legitimacy and the role of the Commission', *Arena Working Paper* no. 3, Oslo.

Mattelart, A. and Palmer, M. (1991) 'Advertising in Europe. Promises, pressures, and pitfalls', *Media, Culture and Society* 13(4): 535–56.

Mazey, S. (1992) 'Conception and evolution of the High Authority's administrative service (1952–1956): from supranational principles to multinational practices' in Heyen, E.V. (ed.) *Yearbook of European administrative history: early European Community administration*, Baden-Baden: Nomos: 31–47.

Mazey, S. and Richardson, J.J. (1995) 'Promiscuous policy-making: the European policy style?' in Rhodes, C. and Mazey, S. (eds) *The state of the European Union vol. 3: building a European Polity?*, Boulder: Lynne Rienner: 337–59.

McLure, C.E. (1986) 'Tax competition: is what's good for the private goose also good for the public gander?', *National Tax Journal* 39(3) September: 341–8.

McNamara, K.R. (1998) *The currency of ideas. Monetary politics in the European Union*, Ithaca and London: Cornell University Press.

McQuail, D. (1994) *Mass communication theory. An introduction*, London: Sage, 3rd edition.

Meynaud, J. (1969) *Technocracy*, New York: The Free Press.

Monnet, J. (1978) *Memoirs*, London: Collins.

Moravcsik, A. (1998) 'Does international cooperation strengthen the national executives? The case of monetary policy in the European Union', *Paper delivered to the international conference on Europeanization*, European University Institute, 19 June 1998.

Muller, P. (1995) 'Les politiques publiques comme construction d'un rapport au monde' in Faure, A., Pollet, G. and Warin, P. (eds) *La Construction du Sens dans les Politiques Publiques. Débats autour de la Notion de Référentiel*, Paris: L'Harmattan: 153–79.

Mundell, R. (1961) 'A theory of optimum currency areas', *American Economic Review* 51(4) September: 657–65.

Obradovic, D. (1996) 'Policy legitimacy in the European Union', *Journal of Common Market Studies* 34(2) June: 191–221.

OECD (1997) *The OECD report on regulatory reform*, Paris: OECD Publications.

Offe, C. (1992) 'Designing institutions for East European transitions', *Paper prepared for the institutional design conference*, The Australian National University, Research School of Social Science, 7–8 December.

Padoa-Schioppa, T. (1988) 'The EMS: a long term view' in Giavazzi, F., Micossi, S. and Milner, M. (eds) *The European Monetary System*, Cambridge: Cambridge University Press: 369–84.

Padoa-Schioppa, T. (1994) *The road to Monetary Union in Europe. The emperor, the kings, and the genies*, Oxford: Clarendon Press.

Page, E. (1997) *People who run Europe*, Oxford: Oxford University Press.

Pedler, R.H. and Schaefer, G.F. (1996) (eds) *Shaping European law and policy. The role of committees and comitology in the political process*, Maastricht: European Institute of Public Administration.

Peschek, J.G. (1987) *Policy-planning organizations: elite agendas and America's rightward turn*, Philadelphia: Temple University Press.

Peters, G.B. (1992) 'Bureaucratic politics and the institutions of the European Community' in Sbragia, A. (ed.) *Europolitics. Institutions and policy-making in the 'new' European Community*, Washington: Brookings: 75–122.

Peters, G.B. (1994) 'Agenda-setting in the European Community', *Journal of European Public Policy* 1(1): 9–26.

Peters, G.B. and Barker, A. (1993) (eds) *Advising West European governments. Inquiries, expertise and public policy*, Pittsburgh: University of Pittsburgh Press.

Peterson, J. (1995a) 'EU research policy: the politics of expertise' in Rhodes, C. and Mazey, S. (eds) *The State of the European Union vol. 3: building a European polity?*, Harlow: Longman: 391–411.

Peterson, J. (1995b) 'Decision-making in the European Union: towards a framework for analysis', *Journal of European Public Policy* 2(1): 69–93.

Phelps, E. (1968) 'Money wage dynamics and labour market equilibrium', *Journal of Political Economy* 76(2) July–August: 678–711.

Phillips, A.W. (1958) 'The relationship betweeen unemployment and the rate of change of money wages in the United Kingdom, 1861–1957', *Economica* 25 November: 283–99.

Picciotto, S. (1992) *International business taxation. A study in the internationalization of business regulation*, London: Weidenfeld and Nicolson.

Pigou, A.C. (1932) *The economics of welfare*, London: Macmillan (1st edition: 1920).

Pollack, M. (1997) 'Delegation, agency, and agenda setting in the European Community', *International Organization* 51(1) Winter: 99–134.

Powell, W.W. and DiMaggio, P. (1991) (eds) *The new institutionalism in organizational analysis*, Chicago: University of Chicago Press.

Putnam, R.D. (1976) *The comparative study of political elites*, Englewood Cliffs: Prentice-Hall.

165

Putnam, R.D. (1977) 'Elite transformation in advanced industrial societies: an empirical assessment of the theory of technocracy', *Comparative Political Studies* **10**(3) October: 383–412.

Putnam, R.D. (1988) 'Diplomacy and domestic politics': the logic of two-level games', *International Organization* **42**(2): 427–60.

Radaelli, C.M. (1995) 'The role of knowledge in the policy process', *Journal of European Public Policy* **2**(2): 160–83.

Radaelli, C.M. (1997) *The politics of corporate taxation in the European Union. Knowledge and international policy agendas*, London: Routledge.

Radaelli, C.M. (1998) 'Governing European regulation. The challenges ahead', *Robert Schuman Centre Policy Paper* no. 3–98, Florence: European University Institute.

Radaelli, C.M. and Dente, B. (1996) 'Evaluation strategies and the analysis of the policy process', *Evaluation* **2**(1): 51–66.

Rhodes, R.A.W. (1997) *Understanding governance. Policy networks, governance, reflexivity and accountability*, Buckingham: Open University Press.

Richardson, J.J. (1996) 'Policy-making in the EU: ideas and garbage-cans of primeval soup' in Richardson, J.J. (ed.) *The European Union: power and policy-making*, London: Routledge: 3–23.

Rochefort, D.A. and Cobb, R. (1994) (eds) *The politics of problem definition*, Lawrence: University Press of Kansas.

Rose, R. (1991) 'What is lesson-drawing?', *Journal of Public Policy* **11**: 3–30.

Rose, R. (1993) *Lesson-drawing in public policy*, Chatham (NJ): Chatham House Publishers.

Rosen, S. (1973) (ed.) *Testing the theory of the military-industrial complex*, Lexington (MA): Lexington Books.

Rosenthal, G.G. (1975) *The men behind the decisions. Cases in European policy-making*, Lexington (MA): Lexington Books.

Rudig, W. (1992) 'Sources of technological controversy. Proximity to or alienation from technology?' in Barker, A. and Peters, G.B. (eds) *The politics of expert advice*, Pittsburgh: University of Pittsburgh Press: 17–32.

Sabatier, P.A. (1993) 'Policy change over a decade or more' in Sabatier, P.A. and Jenkins-Smith, H.C. (eds) *Policy change and learning. An advocacy coalition approach*, Boulder: Westview: 13–39.

Sabatier, P.A. (1998) 'The advocacy coalition framework: revisions and relevance for Europe', *Journal of European Public Policy* **5**(1) March: 98–130.

Sala-i-Martin, X. and Sachs, J. (1992) 'Fiscal federalism and optimum currency areas: evidence for Europe' in Canzoneri, M.B. and Grilli, V. (eds) *Establishing a Central Bank. Issues in Europe and lessons from the US*, Cambridge: Cambridge University Press, 195–219.

Sanchez-Tabernero, A., Denton, A., Lochon, P.-Y., Mounier, P., and Wolt, R. (1993) *Media concentration in Europe. Commercial enterprise and the public interest*, Dusseldorf: European Institute for the Media.

Sandholtz, W. (1993) 'Choosing union: monetary politics and Maastricht', *International Organization* 47(1): 1–39.

Sandholtz, W. (1996) 'Money troubles. Europe's rough road to Monetary Union', *Journal of European Public Policy* 3(1): March 84–101.

Sartori, G. (1987) *The theory of democracy revisited* Chatham, New Jersey: Chatham House Publishers.

Scharpf, F.W. (1996) 'Negative and positive integration in the political economy of European welfare states' in Marks, G., Scharpf, F.W., Schmitter, P. and Streeck, W. (eds), *Governance in the European Union*, London: Sage: 15–39.

Schmidt, S.K. and Werle, R. (1998) *Coordinating technology. Studies in the international standardization of telecommunications*, London and Cambridge: The MIT Press.

Schmitter, P. (1998) *How to democratize the European Union.* Unpublished typescript, to appear (in Italian) as *Come e perchè democratizzare l'unione europea*, Bologna: Il Mulino, 1999.

Scolve, R.E. (1995) *Democracy and technology*, New York: Guilford.

Shapiro, M. (1997) 'The problems of independent agencies in the United States and the European Union', *Journal of European Public Policy* 2(1): 276–91.

Siebert, F., Peterson, T. and Schramm, W. (1956) *Four theories of the press*, Chicago and London: University of Illinois Press.

Sinn, H.W. (1990) 'Tax harmonisation and tax competition in Europe', *European Economic Review* 34: 489–504.

Steinmo, S. (1993) *Taxation and democracy. Swedish, British and American approaches to financing the modern state*, New Haven and London: Yale University Press.

Stevens, A. and Stevens, H. (1996) 'The non-management of Europe', *Paper prepared for the 8th conference on the Europeanisation of public policy*, 20–21 June, Paris.

Stone, D., Denham, A. and Garnett, M. (1998) (eds) *Think tanks across the world. A comparative perspective*, Manchester: Manchester University Press.

Tanzi, V. (1995) *Taxation in an integrating world*, Washington: Brookings.

Tanzi, V. and Bovenberg, A.L. (1990) 'Is there a need for harmonising capital income taxes within EC countries?' in Siebert, H. (ed.) *Reforming capital income taxation*, Tubingen: J.B. Mohr: 171–96.

Thurow, L. (1981) *The zero sum society: distribution and the possibilities for economic change*, New York: Basic Books.

Tiebout, C. (1956) 'A pure theory of local expenditures', *Journal of Political Economy* (64): 416–24.

Touraine, A. (1974) *The post-industrial society*, London: Wildwood House.

Tsoukalis, L. (1977) *The politics and economics of European Monetary integration*, London: Allen and Unwin.

UNICE (Union of Industrial and Employers' Confederations of Europe) (1998) Company taxation in the single market: A business perspective, Brussels, 4 November, typescript.

Veblen, T. (1963) *The engineers and the price system*, New York: Harcourt Brace and World, Inc. (original edition by Viking Press, 1921).

Veljanovski, C. (1989) (ed.) *Freedom in broadcasting*, London: Institute of Economic Affairs.

Verdun, A. (1997) 'The role of the Delors Committee in the creation of EMU: an epistemic community?' *Paper prepared for presentation at the 5th biennial international conference of the European Community Studies Association*, 29 May–1 June, Seattle, USA.

Verdun, A. (1999) 'The role of the Delors Committee in the creation of EMU: an epistemic community', *Journal of European Public Policy* 6(2): Forthcoming.

Vinals, J. (1996) 'European monetary integration: a narrow or a wide EMU?' *European Economic Review* 40: 1103–9.

Walker, J.L. (1969) 'The diffusion of innovations among the American States', *American Political Science Review*, 63 September: 880–99.

Wallace, W. and Smith, J. (1995) 'Democracy or technocracy? European integration and the problem of popular consent', *West European Politics* 18(3): 137–57.

Weatherford, S.M. (1992) 'Measuring political legitimacy', *American Political Science Review* 86(1) March: 149–65.

Webb, M.C. (1996) 'International cooperation and the taxation of transnational business: the OECD and the EU', *Paper prepared for delivery at the 1996 Annual Meeting of the American Political Science Association*, August 29–September 1, San Francisco.

Weiler, J.H.H. (1992) 'After Maastricht: Community legitimacy in post-1992 Europe' in Adams, W.J. (ed.) *Singular Europe: economy and policy of the EC after 1992*, Ann Arbor: University of Michigan Press: 11–41.

Weiss, C.H. (1979) 'The many meanings of research utilization', *Public Administration Review*, 39(5): 426–31.

Wildavsky, A. (1987) *The art and craft of policy analysis*, New Brunswick, NJ: Transaction Books (1st edition: 1979).

Williams, R. (1971) *Politics and technology*, Basingstoke: Macmillan.

Wittrock, B. (1982) 'Social knowledge, public policy and social betterment. A review of current research on knowledge utilization in policy-making', *European Journal of Political Research* 10: no. 1, March 83–9.

Wolton, D. (1992) 'Values and normative choices in French television' in Blulmer, J. (ed.) *Television and the public interest. Vulnerable values in West European broadcasting*, London: Sage: 147–60.

Yin, R.K. (1994) *Case study research*, London: Sage, 2nd edition.

Zee, H.H. (1996) 'Taxation and unemployment', *IMF working paper*, no. 45–96, Washington: International Monetary Fund.

Zito, A. (1998) 'Epistemic communities and European integration', *Paper prepared for ECPR Workshop no. 22 on 'The role of ideas in policy-making'*, European Consortium for Political Research 26th Joint Sessions of Workshops, University of Warwick, Coventry, UK, 23–8 March.

Index

advocacy coalitions, 38, 42–43
  beliefs 42, 50, 123, 148
  media policy, 123–124, 140–144
  tax policy, 98, 107
agenda-setting, 39, 49
Akin, William, 18, 19, 20
Allison, Graham, 38
Amato, Giuliano, 51, 60
Amsterdam European Council, 111
Andersen, Svein, 3, 33, 34, 154
Armstrong, Kenneth, 123
Attinà, Fulvio, 50
Australia, 24, 68

Bacon, Francis, 6, 14
Balladur, Edouard, 60, 61, 62, 82
Balzac, Honore de, 29
Bangemann, Martin, 131, 132
Bank of Italy, 2
Barre, Raymond, 56, 81
Barzanti, Roberto, 125
Bayern, 148
Beetham, David, 52
Belgium, 57, 65, 85
Bell, Daniel, 17, 21, 22
Beltrame, Francesca, 146
Berlin, 148
Blumler, Jay, 118
Bulmer, Simon, 123
Brandt, Willy, 57
Brittan, Leon, 131, 132
Bundesbank, 60, 62, 63, 64, 69, 70,
  75, 79, 84
Bundeskartellamt, 139
bureaucratic politics, 38–40, 48–49,
  79, 124, 136, 144–145, 153
Burnham, James, 20–21
Burns, Tom, 3, 33, 34, 154
Burris, Beverly, 12

Calvet, Jacques, 4
Cameron, David, 62, 63, 74, 75, 76
Canada, 67, 83
Cassese, Sabino, 32
Chirac, Jacques, 2
citizens, 3, 31, 43, 69, 78, 79, 85,
  117, 132
  see also public opinion
citizens first (programme of the
  Commission), 3
Colombo, Emilio, 82
Commission, European, 1, 2, 3, 4, 7,
  8, 9, 32, 33, 35, 36, 37, 38, 39,
  42, 43, 44, 45, 47, 48, 56, 61,
  65, 72, 73, 76, 87, 88, 89, 91,
  92, 93, 94, 95, 96, 97, 98, 99,
  100, 102, 103, 104, 105, 106,
  107, 108, 109, 110, 113, 119,
  124, 125, 126, 127, 128, 129,
  130, 131, 132, 133, 135, 136,
  137, 138, 139, 140, 142, 143,
  144, 145, 150, 151, 152, 155
Comte, Auguste, 14–15, 22, 29, 150
Confédération Fiscale Européenne, 97
Corvaja, Giuseppe, 29
Council of Ministers, 2, 32, 35, 38,
  39, 40, 43, 47, 49, 56, 60, 61,
  62, 72, 73, 88, 92, 93, 94, 95,
  97, 98, 99, 100, 102, 106, 112,
  113, 121, 126, 130, 131, 134,
  155
Czarniawska, Barbara, 52

della Cananea, Giacinto, 32
Delors, Jacques, 1, 4, 54, 61, 62, 64,
  73, 75, 77, 79
Denmark, 1, 54
Department of National Heritage,
  139

Department of Trade and Industry, 139
DiMaggio, Paul, 44, 52
Dogan, Mattei, 52
Dolowitz, David, 52
Downs, Anthony, 38
Drake, helen, 52
Dyson, Kenneth, 54, 69, 71, 73, 75, 77

Economic and Monetary Union (EMU), 1–3, 45, 53–84, 109, 110, 138, 150–151
   Ashford Castle meeting, 63, 84
   bankers, 46, 55, 62, 72, 73–77, 80
   chronology of events, 56–65
   Delors Committee, 46, 62, 73–80, 84
   economic policy paradigms, 67–73, 150
   economic rationale, 64–67, 108
   economists versus monetarists, 56–58
   European Monetary System (EMS), 59–61, 82
   Franco-German axis, 61, 68–69, 79–80, 84
   Hanover European Council, 62, 73, 75, 77
   optimum currency areas, 67
   Phillips curve, 69, 83
   political business cycle, 70–71
   snake, 59
   The Hague summit, 56
   Werner Report, 56–58, 67, 81, 92, 93
Economic and Social Committee, 127
Eichengreen, Barry, 81
Egan, Michelle, 50
Ellul, Jacques, 22–23
Engels, Friedrich, 14
epistemic communities, 38, 40–43, 47–49, 153
   and coalitions, 41–42
   and Economic and Monetary Union, 55, 73–77, 79–80
   and media policy, 145
   and policy transfer, 45–46
   and tax policy, 98
Eurobarometer, 3
European Central Bank, 2, 7, 53, 62, 63, 64, 65, 67, 69, 72, 153, 154
   see also Economic and Monetary Union
European Commission, see Commission, European

European Company Statute, 92, 99
European Court of Justice, 47, 88–89, 99, 122, 125, 126, 134, 136–137, 143
European Parliament, 4, 38, 39, 40, 43, 47, 72, 125, 126, 127, 128, 130, 131, 132, 134, 140, 141, 144, 145, 146, 147, 150, 153, 154, 155
evaluation studies, 29, 155–156
experts (and policy-making), 4, 7, 24, 31–33, 36, 47–48, 93, 95, 100, 111, 114
   see also epistemic communities

Fayot, Ben, 130
Featherstone, Kevin, 31, 32, 69, 73, 75, 77
Fédération des Experts Comptables Européens, 97
Ferkiss, Christopher, 22
Fischer, Frank, 16, 23
Fisichella, Domenico, 27, 29
forum politics, 42–43, 93
France, 2, 14, 33, 53, 57, 60, 61, 62, 68, 69, 72, 75, 76, 79, 84, 120, 141
Friedman, Milton, 81

Galbraith, John, 21
Garrett, Geoffrey, 81
General Agreement on Tariffs and Trade, 129
Genscher, Hans Dietrich, 60, 61
Germany, 2, 23, 53, 57, 58, 59, 60, 61, 62, 63, 68, 69, 71, 72, 75, 76, 79, 80, 82, 84, 101, 105, 109, 120, 138, 139, 140, 142
Giavazzi, franco, 82
Gormley, William, 37
Grauwe, Paul de, 84
Great depression, 18, 19
Greece, 3, 60, 65

Haas, Peter, 40, 41, 74
Habermas, Jurgen, 28
Hamburg, 148
Harcourt, Alison, 38, 116, 128, 136, 146
Heclo, Hugh, 122
High Authority, 31–33, 50
Hix, Simon, 156
Hoffmann-Riem, Wolfgang, 146
Hudig, Dirk, 114
Humphreys, Peter, 146

Institute for Fiscal Studies, 96
Institute of Chartered Accountants, 97
International Monetary Fund, 96
Ireland, 59, 60
isomorphism, (see policy transfer)
Italy, 2, 23, 57, 60, 62, 65, 68, 72, 79, 102, 113, 119, 120, 126

Johnson, Lindon, 29

Keynes, John M., 14
Khol, Helmut, 61, 62, 63, 75, 76, 79, 105
Kingdon, John, 131
Kohler-Koch, Beate, 156
knowledge utilization, 27, 29

Law Society, 97
learning, 39–43, 48, 49, 68–69, 78, 94, 140, 143, 144
League of nations, 50
legitimacy, 25
  democratic legitimacy, 43, 78
  technocratic legitimacy, 43–46, 78–79, 93, 107–110, 137–140, 150–151
  see also policy transfer
Lord, Christopher, 52
Luxembourg, 56, 57, 62, 85, 106, 114, 117, 119, 120

McNamara, Katlhleen R., 81
McQuail, Denis, 145
Majone, GianDomenico, 35, 36, 156
Marcussen, Martin, 67
Marsh, David, 52
Martin, Lisa, 81
Matlary, Janne Haaland, 52
Mazey, Sonia, 33
media ownership policy, 116–148, 149, 151, 152–153
  audience share, 130, 136, 138
  competition policy, 122, 132–136
  concentration, 120–121
  convergence, 129, 135, 142–143
  EU external policy, 129
  governance regime, 123, 125–137
  protocol to Amsterdam Treaty, 119, 137, 143
  normative theories, 116–117
  pluralism, 117, 124, 128, 140–141, 145

single market approach, 128, 132, 140–142, 144
merger regulation, 133–134, 136
Miert, Karel van, 136
Mitterrand, François, 61, 62, 63, 68
Monnet, Jean 31–33, 36, 40, 50
Monti, Mario, 102, 111, 114, 130, 131, 132, 136, 140, 142, 143, 148
Muller, Pierre, 41

Netherlands, 57, 58, 62, 65
Neumark, Fritz, 89
'new class' theorists, 23
new deal, 19
New Zealand, 68
North-Rhein Westfalia, 148

Obradovic, daniela, 52
Offe, Claus, 45, 151
Oreja, Marcelino, 131
Organization for Economic Cooperation and Development, 96, 114, 141

parliaments
  parliamentary representation, 33–34
  post-parliamentary governance, 3, 154
  see also European Parliament
Padoa-Schioppa, Tommaso, 61
Pagano, Marco 50
Page, Edward, 50, 51, 52, 154
Peters, Guy, 38, 39
Piris, Jean-Claude, 5
Plato, 12, 13
Pöhl, Karl Otto, 63, 75
policy transfer, 43–46, 149
  differences between EMU and tax policy, 107–109
  and diffusion, 52
  and EMU, 78–79, 150–151
  and media policy, 137–140, 151
  and tax policy, 107–110, 151
political decision-making, 49, 55, 79–80, 102, 107, 111–112, 127, 145, 152–156
Pompidou, George, 57
Portugal, 60
positive and negative integration, 90, 112, 119, 120, 129, 140, 143
Powell, Walter, 44, 52
progressive movement, 16

public opinion, 1, 47, 54, 117
  see also citizens
Putnam, Robert, 3, 23, 25

Radaelli, Claudio M., 51
regulation (and EU public policy), 7,
  33–38, 46, 149, 152, 153
representation (mechanisms of), 33–34
Richardson, Jeremy, 41, 42
Rosenthal, Glenda, 58
Ruding, Wolfgang, 28
Ruding, Onno, 100

Sabatier, Paul, 42, 51, 123
Sanchez-Tabernero, Alfonzo, 146
Sandholtz, Wayne, 54, 81
Saint-Simon, Claude-Henry de, 6,
  14–15, 17, 18, 22, 29
Santer, Jacques, 130, 132
Sartori, Giovanni, 13, 14, 25
Saxony, 148
Scharpf, Fritz, 113
Schinzel, Dieter, 130
Schleswig-Holstein, 148
Schumpeter, Joseph, 14
Scott, Howard, 18
Scrivener, Christiane, 94, 106
Segrè, Claudio, 91, 93
Shapiro, Martin, 50
Single European Act, 95, 96, 111,
  126
Smith, Julie, 31
Spain, 2, 60, 79, 84
state aid, 106
Steinmo, Sven, 114
Stendhal, 29
Stoltenberg, Gerhard, 60
Switzerland, 114

tax policy, 85–115, 138, 151, 152
  capital export neutrality, 96
  capital import neutrality, 96
  direct corporate tax measures
    (1990), 98–99
  economic rationale, 108–109
  effective tax rates, 95–97
  employment, 104, 111, 112
  McDougall Report, 113
  Neumark Committee Report,
    89–91, 112
  Ruding Committee Report,
    100–102, 103, 114
  systems for taxing profits, 86–87,
    91

Segrè Committee Report, 92
tax competition, 85–86, 91,
  101–102, 103–107, 108, 154
tax discrimination, 85, 89, 102
tax neutrality, 91, 96–98, 104, 107,
  108
tax treaties, 99
(van den) Tempel study (taxation of
  profits), 92
transfer pricing, 98, 99
Taylor, Frederick, 16, 18
technocracy
  conceptual limitations, 26–28, 47,
    149
  definition, 11, 12
  history of the concept, 13–24
  ideology, 15, 16, 20, 25
  mentality, 25, 37
  normative analysis, 28
  old and new, 24
  see also legitimacy
technocracy
  and EMU, 54–55, 58–59, 77–80
  and European Union policy process,
    46–47
  and media policy, 124, 125–127,
    140–145
  and origins of the European
    Community, 30–33
  and policy sciences, 24
  and power, 24
  and tax policy, 87, 88, 93, 94–102,
    104–105, 107, 111, 112
  and traditional elites, 23, 31
  and state planning, 21, 46–47
  see also legitimacy
Technocrats (American movement,
  1900–1941), 18–20
technology, 6, 8, 12, 19
technostructure, 21–22, 33, 47
Thatcher, Margaret, 62, 84
think tanks, 24, 26, 28, 96
Thüringen, 148
Tongue, Carole, 131
Touraine, Alain, 16
treaties, 1–3, 5, 31, 50, 53, 54, 55,
  65, 72, 79, 88, 89, 108, 109,
  119, 128, 133, 143, 155, 156
  see also Economic and Monetary
    Union
Tsoukalis, Louis, 57, 81

uncertainty, 40–41, 44–45, 47–49,
  97, 107

UNICE (Union of Industrial and Employers' Confederations of Europe), 95, 114
United Kingdom, 23, 24, 60, 62, 63, 73, 76, 77, 101, 119, 126, 138, 139, 140, 142
United Nations, 50
United States of America, 24, 67, 83, 129
  diffusion of technocratic ideas, 16–21, 29

Veblen, Thorstein, 17–18
  Veblen's soviet of technicians, 18, 24

Veljanovski, Cento, 146
Verdun, Amy, 54, 74, 75, 76, 81

Wallace, William, 31
Weatherford, Stephen, 52
Weaver, Vernon, 147
Weber, Max, 15
Webb, Michael, 104
Weiler, Joseph, 52
Werner, Pierre, 56
  see also Economic and Monetary Union
Wildavsky, Aaron, 110
Williamson, David, 2
World Trade Organization, 129, 141